GOING
BUDDHIST

GOING
BUDDHIST

Panic and emptiness, the Buddha and me

PETER J CONRADI

✳ SHORT BOOKS

First published in 2004 by
Short Books
15 Highbury Terrace
London N5 1UP

10 9 8 7 6 5 4 3

A CIP catalogue record for this book
is available from the British Library.

ISBN 1-904095-63-1

Printed in Great Britain by
Mackays of Chatham Ltd, Kent.

For Iris Murdoch
15 July 1919 – 8 February 1999

CONTENTS

PREFACE

A recent article in *New Scientist*, widely quoted in the British press, "proved" that the left prefrontal lobe of the brain, "associated with positive emotions, good moods, foresight, planning and self-control" is unusually active among committed Buddhists. A Professor at Duke University called these results "tantalising". He added: "We can now hypothesise with some confidence that those apparently happy, calm Buddhist souls really are happy." (This is a view that would not have surprised the author, in 1959, of a book called *Christ and Freud*: ..."in comparison with what obtains in Christian countries, the neuroses are of far less incidence in Buddhist and Hindu communities...")

These scientists represent one kind of witness. Often Buddhist meditation has been seen as at best a harmless mystical preoccupation, at worst a socially irresponsible self-indulgence. In the USA today 5 million are Buddhist; in Europe estimates vary between one million and four, depending upon whether you factor in all refugees from Asia, some of whom are nominal Buddhists only. The UK has around a hundred Tibetan centres, as well as 90 Theravada, and then some 40 Zen, and lastly a further hundred or so other groups including Friends of the Western Buddhist Order.

An audience for the Dalai Lama's teaching recently filled Wembley Conference Centre for three days. Celebrities such as Richard Gere, Tina Turner, John Cleese and Steven Seagal have been claimed for it. And another scientist, Albert Einstein, wrote that it has "the characteristics of what would be expected in a cosmic religion for the future": transcending a personal God, avoiding dogma and theology, covering both the natural and the spiritual, and based on the experience of all things as a meaningful unity.

Is Einstein accurate? Like many Buddhists, I often spend a month meditating for eight or ten silent hours a day with a group – being without *babble* is restful – I often travel to study with meditation masters, and sometimes get asked how this started. What follows is an attempt to give a few answers, not least to myself.

Finding the ox's traces

STAGE FRIGHT

Iris Murdoch asks, alarmingly, "Are you a religious person?" Autumn 1982, misty; evenings dark early and cold. Our first solo talk: her first question. We are drinking pints of beer in an Edinburgh pub. She is 63; I am 37. Feeling an intellectual's routine contempt for the religions I'd met – pie-in-the-sky, opium-for-the-masses, bigotry and persecution of heresy – I try to consider her question. I know that she dismisses the idea of instantaneous change (the quick fix, the one-shot deal) as a modern lie. She sees life as a long quest, search, pilgrimage. A title sighted in a bookshop window – *Good News for Modern Man* – seemed to me (by contrast with such piety) highly comical. There is no good news for modern man. Just an unappeased hunger to know what meaning a life might have. "Are you a religious person?" she asks. I cannot reply.

Iris is giving the ten Gifford lectures in Natural Theology which rotate between Scottish University cities. She has found it hard to organize her thoughts, and over a fortnight the audience of good Morningside and Newington ladies has been shrinking. But I am a devout listener, who loves her fiction with its fantastic realism and holy fools, have been struck by her urgent belief that everyday consciousness consists in low, self-centred states of illusion, and electrified by her assertion that day that, by contrast, "the good man *literally* sees a different world from the bad or mediocre man…" Here is a revolutionary way of thinking: not merely behaviour, but *perception itself* would shift, if moral change occurred. She wants to know how one changes, and advocates cultivating a "passionate, stilled attention" so that one watches – she quoted Rilke on Cézanne – "*as a dog watches*".

She catechises me that night because I have already elected her my mentor. Finding myself lodged in an adjacent room to hers at the Edinburgh staff club, I had a day earlier fled to the Raeburn Hotel. A flight from the enchanter perhaps? I am writing a doctorate on Iris's

Platonism (published as *The Saint and the Artist*), and do not want to invade her privacy. Ironic today: twenty years later I would research and publish a so-called "full and frank" biography of her. She is plump and short with dishevelled hair, exhausted from lecturing, her face open with tenderness and compassion like a mollusc, yet also deeply private, with an intense *pudeur* and a steely strength. She wears a pie-crust-collared white blouse inside a flowery tunic. I wait so long trying to decide how to answer her question about whether or not I am religious – flummoxed – that she shifts her ground. "Give me a *resumé* – put me in the picture, as it were." And soon: "Describe your house." I try to oblige.

Her own religious position interested me. The description in her novel *The Bell* of characters "disturbed and hunted by God, able to live neither in nor out of the world" was true of her, too. She called herself a Christian-Buddhist. She could never relinquish Christianity, yet was dismayed by its stubborn, futile insistence on the literal rather than figurative truth of its myths – Virgin Birth and Resurrection. She wanted these to survive as instructive and truth-bearing stories that had after all, together with classical mythology, inspired many of the glories in Western art and literature, but not to be sole pre-requisites of faith itself.

"It is certain because it is impossible" (*Certum est quia impossible est*), wrote the 2nd century Christian scholar Tertullian. An attitude satirised by Lewis Carroll:

"I can't believe that!" said Alice.

"Can't you?" the Queen said in a pitying tone. "Try again: draw a long breath, and shut your eyes."

Alice laughed. "There's no use trying," she said: "one can't believe impossible things."

"I daresay you haven't had much practice," said the Queen. "When I was your age, I always did it for half-an-hour a day. Why, sometimes I've believed as many as six impossible things before breakfast."

Christian duty to believe six impossible things before breakfast was, Iris feared, helping kill off the essential: Christ's ethical vision, that we must love one another. Perhaps she viewed all religions with a certain passionate suspicion. "Up *any* religion a man may climb," one of her characters observes. But she was not a "joiner". Buddhism got close to the perennial philosophy she sought, a set of ancient techniques for perceiving less selfishly. Her own early life (I much later discovered) had taught her about selfishness and its harvest and she sought to learn to live with care.

She wanted Buddhism none the less to educate Christianity, to create a non-supernatural religion, with Christ the Buddha of the West: a man neither Virgin-born nor resurrected, who became enlightened, and whose life was – in itself – a kind of teaching. God and the after-life were – for her – infantile bribes. The sooner both were dropped, the better. Indeed "God" himself was an essentially anti-religious idea: we have to be "good for nothing", without hope of reward. This brought her close to those great Christian mystics for whom the dogmas of Christianity were secondary, and close, also, to Buddhism, the only great world religion without belief in a Creator, where individual experience (as for the mystics) counts for much. For Buddhists there is no one to save us or to blame. The practitioner has to do the thing alone. Iris wanted meditation to be taught in schools, and recommended to me two authors, one – D.T. Suzuki – who wrote on Zen, the other – John Blofield – about the picturesque and magical Buddhism of Tibet. Westerners have long believed Tibet holds a secret that might help cure their ills. Not all of these have been as foolish as the co-founder of theosophy, Madame

Blavatsky, starry-eyed about all good news from the East.

One week later I hit upon a possible answer to her question about religion. We are in an Italian restaurant. The waiter stands in greeting behind her chair, his arms about her, kisses her head. Had she heard his troubles on an earlier occasion, listening to him faithfully "as a dog listens"? She seems pleased to see him too. In that day's lecture she had explained that she used to consider the mother as the paradigm good person, but now sees maternity as complicit with power. She has therefore switched to aunts. She had known some good aunts but *no good uncles*.

"The task is to love other people, and possibly *dogs*… *Aunts* show that the thing can be done."

P.G.Wodehouse took another view: "It is no use telling me that there are good aunts and bad aunts. At the core, they are all alike. Sooner or later, out pops the cloven hoof," says Bertie Wooster, who hopes that Turkey might be a country where aunts, sewn into sacks, might regularly be dropped into the Bosphorus. Yet if Wodehouse had ever created a good aunt other than Aunt Dahlia, it might have been someone like Iris : she seems a good, brusque because shy, highly intuitive aunt herself, full of affections, and shrewd about others.

I had decided to explore Buddhism. The "illumination of the Guru", the psychologist Antony Storr believes, often follows a period of acute psychological distress. This was my experience. And Storr is right that the spiritual search can provoke new delusions, self-worship, solipsism. Iris's fiction turns such delusions, follies and hypocrisies into a divine comedy of her own; novels such as *The Time of the Angels* show those who cease to believe in God starting to believe not in nothing, but in *anything*.

Storr's equal pathologising of the unhappiness and the ensuing faith, on the other hand, sheds little light. It often takes a crisis to see what a life's shape has been: the heart attack that tells us we live too stressfully or shows what really matters, and what might perhaps now be shed.

Nothing-ness bothered me. Perhaps it is related to what the French mean by *le Trac* or stage-fright, a recognisable life-condition. No longer automatically assuaged by easy sex, my stage-fright had different elements, some nameable. Beyond dealing with a vexed friendship, and divorced parents, and fear of illness, panic floated free of causes. Judging from The Help Overcome Panic Effects Helpline, the No Panic Helpline, the charity HOPE (Help Overcome Panic Effects) (*Evening*

Standard, December 1997) – not to speak of the expensive panic website "fearfighter.com" – big city panic-attacks are common. Sweating, shaking, pain, giddiness, feeling faint from hyperventilation, one's guts locked in painful spasm. Strange animal fright. Solitary confinement. One's head full of accidents, like an expectant mother's. A claustrophobic terror of being abandoned in a desolate place, quite separate, expelled into a void, found out as an interloper, dying-on-the-spot, "falling infinitely". In the most intense panics it is unclear whether dying or continuing to suffer seems worse.

Being itself seemed uncanny. Or as the German language wittily has it, "*Un-heimlich*", in some sense not-at-home. I did not understand how to start to feel at home on the planet. Anxiety is a task, an occupation, a career. As much as they define characters in Kafka or Sebald's fictions (one named *Vertigo*), fear and trembling were my special subjects; I could have majored in panic. Consciousness itself sometimes seemed to be a species of anxiety-disorder. This must be true for many: 22 million prescriptions were written for tranquillisers in the UK in 2000. Even falling asleep can be hard, doubting the safety-zone that catches and holds us once we fall.

Perhaps panic resembles "cutting" – using a knife to damage oneself: it can feel self-inflicted, hard to stop. What exactly are we? Since I'm mortal, what sustains me in existence? How is there a world, something rather than nothing? What *sense* is to be found? Does any explanation cover the facts without going way beyond them, without what A.J. Ayer called "woolly uplift"? How are living and dying done? How might one become available to oneself, and to others?

Philip Larkin wrote a brief, child-like, sinister poem ("Days") in which asking questions about why we are here "brings the priest and the doctor/ in their long coats/ running over the fields." Deep enquiry damages your health. "We're here because we're here," as the old song has it, "thrown into existence" (Heidegger) without consultation.

Fear and courage interested Iris. She spoke of the courage of Vladimir Bukovsky, who had exposed Soviet abuse of psychiatric hospitals where dissident free spirits, himself included, were tortured. He had just escaped to the West, helped by a committee that included Iris. Contemplating Bukovsky's courage, her eyes filled. When I raised the subject of "panic", by contrast, she remembered that a Japanese friend observed during an earthquake his saintly Zen companion become (so she reported) nearly invisible, retreating into inner calm.

There was in those years as always no shortage of topics inspiring horror. In Northern Ireland terrorists chain-sawed a man's hand off. Some time before, and after two years planning, the murderer and post-office thief Donald Neilson (the "Black Panther") had kidnapped and tethered Leslie Whittle with a five-foot length of steel piano wire around her neck, on a narrow ledge in an underground pit in the flood drainage shaft system of Bathpool Park. She was found dead without perceptible physical injury. This was impressive. We now know that Whittle died quickly by automatic physical response to high blood pressure in her carotid artery, induced by wire-pressure when she overbalanced, trying to escape. But one alarming account then reported that she had died of terror, caused by "vagal inhibition". Perhaps your mind could – *by itself* – kill you? Fearing dying (especially) on the Northern line I hyper-ventilated into a paper-bag to calm down.

Meanwhile, a new disease, Aids, and a great cull was coming. We froze in anticipation. Another Great War, new generations going "over the top". Who was infected? It was clearer than before that we were all visitors, all guests on the planet. Which of us was going to die a painful and fairly public death ? Only when the first close friend started dying, six years later, did I and my partner decide to have the test. I sat on my meditation cushion that morning, trying dispassionately to watch the bandits of hope and fear before returning to the clinic for the result. "I'm relieved to be able to tell you you're Sero-Negative" or, alternatively, "I'm sorry to have to tell you you're Sero-positive" – switched places in my head. Soon fellow-Buddhists were among the many sickening from AIDS. Two died: it was heartening to see the small community rallying and helping, with tact, and care.

As for my own case, I could impersonate an efficient adult. Malaise, however, continued. In these different and unrelated troubles I pulled off the shelf a book cumbrously entitled *Cutting Through Spiritual Materialism*. Hitherto unread, I had bought it in 1978 when an exchange Professor at Colorado University. I had been living in Boulder not far from the author of this book, a Tibetan called Chögyam Trungpa. Indeed I had idly tried meditation in the same new-age spirit in which, like many visitors, I attempted cross-country skiing. I fell down less often meditating than skiing, but persisted with neither.

I read it at a single, tearful, sitting. Much later an early story from the canon told me about the Buddha comforting the son of a merchant who was sick at heart and crying "Terrifying! Horrible!" in the Deer Park at Varanasi: "It is not terrifying; it is not horrible. Come and sit down... and I will teach you the Dharma [the Way]." The early disciples on gaining instruction often felt that they were being reminded of something they had always half-known, rather than taught something wholly new.

Cutting Through taught me about the Dharma, about the styles of vanity and the fickle monkey-mind that accompanies them. It was not written in the weirdly perfumed museum English of many Dharma translations. It seemed, like much good teaching, to be *about me-as-reader*. It read me, taking me in its stride. It also taught about "Spiritual materialism": any form of religiosity used to create a pay-off, spirituality for purposes of self-aggrandisement or gaining credentials, sugar-coated Dharma, that strengthens egocentricity. "It is important to see that the main point of any spiritual practice is to step out of the bureaucracy of ego," dropping ego's desire "for a higher, more spiritual, more transcendental version of knowledge, religion, virtue, judgement, comfort, or whatever". Iris later approved its author's assertion that "maybe there is no such thing as spirituality" *per se*.

Or perhaps spirituality, if it existed, was that state of mind that might come about when we entirely dropped any desire for it, any attempt to levitate out of our present condition, any desire for "elsewhere". The book's analysis of how ingeniously we keep re-creating new "elsewheres" out of the *idea* of spirituality, is both remorseless and good-humoured. It seems to suggest that the task might consist of trying to do *less* – rather than doing more – than normal, and that such doing less might involve effort.

Moreover, an essentially psychological religion, Buddhism described states of being with uncanny accuracy. The sterile Western philosophy I had met believed that only what was public and measurable was real. It either ignored or discounted the inner life, its proponents arguably terrified by it.

Here, by contrast, was a way of notating and working with mental conditions. Buddhism documented hundreds of states-of-mind with extraordinary fullness and sophistication. It seemed to celebrate a vision of self as – in the first instance – plural and unstable, full of potential. It also suggested the possibility of living in the world in a way that benefited oneself and others.

Back in the Deer Park at Varanasi the Buddha made the merchant's son physically disappear for a while. In my case the experience of reading about the Dharma felt as if someone had wheeled up very close an old-fashioned cannon and fired a large hole through me: the author's understanding directly transmitted, entering the blood-stream like a benign virus, starting a happy reaction. Ecstacy or *Exstasis* literally means to stand outside the self. That is how it felt. Within the newly created space an intense bliss lasted for days, as if I had temporarily shed the burden of self, was free and could fly. All phenomena, both the "good" and the "bad", resembled windfalls or gifts.

I'd found a teacher; and tried to explain to Iris a happy dream-like vision arising spontaneously, whose motto was "Responsible *to* others, not *for* others". The world was not my fault. I could glimpse a path towards absolution from the crime of existing, and so a path to living less blindly. I was not sure how well I communicated this vision of life liberated from exaggerated responsibility (guilt), hence opened up to the possibilities of fresh and real mutuality. She spoke of the Elder Zossima's sense of limitless obligation towards others in

Dostoevsky's *Brothers Karamazov*. I thought this priggish of her and wondered whether, differently understood, guilt might not bring one towards a less neurotic – but not less real – account of one's obligation towards others.

Iris's fiction abounded in characters glimpsing such possible future states of being – what Dame Julian of Norwich termed "*shewings*". Dame Julian was a medieval anchoress or hermit, incarcerated by choice for years in a cell specially built for her adjoining a Norwich church. The states and visions she described, it seems, visit but do not necessarily stay, until we learn how to earn them.

The foolish Effingham Cooper, nearly drowning in the bog in Iris Murdoch's *The Unicorn*, sees that "with the death of the self a perfect love is born". Momentarily his 'I' absented itself. Soon, for both Effingham and me, 'I' returned. Finding a religion can be like falling-in-love – you don't altogether see why you are attracted but believe something within you has shifted none the less. The Buddha's first disciples spoke of "entering the stream" and of the Teachings as truths they had the sensation of *remembering*.

That Pope John Paul II has taken the trouble in his books to attack Buddhism suggests that there might be something valuable here. Why else would he see it as a dangerous rival belief-system? It offers hope to those of us who are hurt by the speed and aggression of the modern world, willing to look within to try to moderate our own aggressive pace and notice that we often run the gauntlet of purely imaginary dangers; or inhabit a fog of no-feeling.

An early Dalai Lama spoke of two ways of dealing with the world's intractability. The commonest strategy was, he saw, equivalent to demanding that the entire planet be covered forthwith with leather. The meditator's response he compared to someone – by contrast – willing instead to re-cover his own shoes. The meditator starts with himself. It may be specially relevant now to Westerners, perishing from the knowingness, nihilism, cynicism of the age as from a lack of oxygen. Like many, I feel this cynicism within me, and not like an alien implant, but as a significant part of my identity.

Buddhism lacks dogmas, even demanding intellectual and personal independence and scepticism in its practitioners. The Buddha enjoined his disciples to take nothing on hearsay, to test the teachings at every point. It is said that the Buddha provides, as it were, merely the recipe for baking warm bread; we have still to bake it afresh each time, ensuring teachings become part of our own experience, anew, as direct inner experience.

This requirement goes so far that one well-known Buddhist book is entitled *If You Meet the Buddha by the Road, Kill Him* – even the Buddha himself is only part of the means to salvation, not a God. Once Buddha has done what he set out to do, he may be discarded. Accordingly one seventeenth-century Japanese Abbot congratulated a peasant-monk who, feeling the cold in winter, chopped up for burning as firewood priceless wooden statues of the Buddha. Even if the story be myth, it is impossible to imagine any European equivalent to this scene; it suggests the distance between Christianity and Buddhism, one literal-minded, dogmatic, superstitious, "historical" and given to fanaticism; the other – relatively speaking – sophisticated, tolerant. When, however, in Japan in the 1960s a Californian hippie tried to repeat the priceless Buddha-burning, this did not go down too well…

Buddhism lacks the caste-consciousness of Hinduism: the humbly-born can meditate too, and the Buddha's "Sangha" or community of monks constituted the world's first democracy, your place in the hierarchy determined not by birth but by length of commitment. Moreover, the Buddha invented monastic life and, despite his own strong initial objections, allowed the first women to be nuns. Later versions of Buddhism (Mahayana, Tantra) suggested that monks and nuns had no monopoly on wisdom. Even householders or people living and working in the world can become enlightened.

Research shows how the meditator's heart rate slows down, brain rhythms alter, and become sensitised to the object of contemplation. One tough comprehensive school which started daily meditation sessions for its children has found its problems declining "with astonishing speed" (*Times*, 2 April 2002).

It seems remarkably *pragmatic*. Its hell-realms not hereafter but here: one of them, the hungry-ghost realm, speaks very directly to our modern condition. Its strange denizens, known as *Pretas*, have fat bellies but tiny necks, and, despite stuffing themselves, never reach satiation: a potent image of consumerism, the neverending pursuit of "durables" that cannot deeply satisfy.

Even its saints are realists and pragmatists. Tibet's best-loved saint, Milarepa – the cotton-clad nettle-eating eleventh-century recluse who attained enlightenment and whose many spontaneously composed songs are still known and learnt and loved today – started adult life as a murderer by black magic of 35 villagers, and had to atone to his teacher by repeatedly building and then, stone-by-stone, taking down a tower.

Milarepa achieved "total awakening in which the object meditated upon, the action of meditating, and the subject who meditates merge into one" so that, he reported, "now I no longer know how to meditate". When he died, his grieving disciples were greatly cheered by one of the phrases from his will suggesting what to do if someone falsely claimed that Milarepa had cared for gold: "*Stuff his mouth with shit.*" They recognised his unique voice.

Milarepa's biographers note *proportionate* results in those who witnessed his life and death. Some instantly achieved higher degrees of realisation. Others went into retreat to try to attain the same level. Even beginners vowed to "abstain from at least one vice and to practise at least one virtue" for life. This seems charmingly practical. The Cambridge-based lama with whom I "took refuge" suggested similarly, and helpfully, that a not ignoble and quite realistic aim of meditation practice is "to *avoid becoming worse on an annual basis*". Iris laughed.

The Tibetan manifestation of Buddhism has other advantages. Its adherents can drink alchohol and are sometimes enjoined to do so – Milarepa's teacher early invited him to drink as did Milarepa to his own Dharma-heir. They also eat meat. Living at or above 14,000 feet, few Tibetans would survive a meat-free diet in winter.

When I next meet Iris in London, lunching at Dino's in South Kensington, her questioning shifts to: "Why Buddhism? Why *fiddle* with the mind?"

She knew I came from an assimilated Jewish family which practised religion in an eccentrically relaxed way. During the only ceremonial Friday night *seder* I remember from my childhood, my mother absent-mindedly cooked for us all a large, delicious cut of roast pork. This was thought a good joke. And Iris knew we were all sent off early to old-fashioned Anglican boarding-schools. "What about Judaism or Christianity" – she added – "so much closer to home?"

Neither Judaism nor Christianity quite addressed the reality of spiritual struggle as I knew it. But by comparison with the Christian religion in which she was brought up, Iris worried that Buddhism was "exotic". Christianity, I riposted, was once as much an Eastern import to these islands as Buddhism is today. To fourth-century Romano-Britons awaiting conversion it must have seemed equally colourful, picturesque and alien, as well as comforting. W.H. Auden pictured its cultish novelty well in his poem "Roman Wall Blues". A centurion, remembering a friend who has "gone" Christian, thinks: "Piso's a Christian, he worships a fish;/ There'd be no kissing if he had his wish."

And isn't exoticism the *point?* Buddhism, especially Tibetan, can still show us what is rugged, raw, uncompromising, magical, terrifying in life – Anglicanism (for many of my friends, at least) can no longer do this. Buddhism holds out a promise of unmediated contact with the essence of things. It seems that extraordinary means are necessary to make us feel ordinary.

But at the same time Jews and Christians take an admirable view of the necessity of charity and of social action from which Buddhists practising in the West can learn: where is Buddhist-Aid to match Christian-Aid (of which, more later)? So I struggle to answer in more detail, aware that my knowledge of Judaism and Christianity – apart from the sublime art the latter has spawned – is shallow.

During the twelve or so hours of fasting and prayer that constitute the Day of Atonement – *Yom Kippur* – I occasionally sat the whole day with my father. Expunging one entire year's misdeeds in a single day seemed cost-efficient and forward-looking. The service was moving.

Indeed, there was a "martyrology" in the afternoon: you remembered what had happened to the Jews during the first and second Exiles; and more recently.

I surveyed the smart, sometimes over-dressed congregation in the Synagogue opposite Lords cricket ground. Many were our stalwart, admirably public-spirited Anglo-Jewish cousins, seemingly wandered in out of a Mark Boxer cartoon – clannish and distinguished-looking relatives "in" timber, in banks, in the City, in tobacco, in the media, in scrap. I had disloyal, treacherous thoughts. The scene recalled the interval at a Viennese opera, the audience in their finery parading on the *Bummel*. And what of the Armenians, Palestinians, Tibetans? Hadn't they suffered as much? Or more? I did not believe my own sense of pathos owed all that much to my Jewishness.

As for Christianity, how did Christians accomplish and embody their excellent ethical ideals? What was the technology? How do you move from "A" to "B"? Prayer? I knew no one to pray to. Not that the C. of E. had strenuous requirements, in terms of belief. It was urbane Lord Melbourne who wittily remarked that religion was all very well *just so long as it did not interfere with your private life. I wanted* to be interfered with.

I certainly misunderstood Christian virtue: it seemed to my ignorant eye to require doing what one least wished to, rather than changing the way one saw the world. Anglicanism looked both messianic, and yet tepid. Messianic beliefs are classic symptoms – when held by one person – of delusional behaviour. When millions hold them they are called religions. If, during endless, boring, pointless Anglican school services – chapel twice a day on Sundays – I was found reading more interesting matter, a beating followed. School sermons rendered *Beyond the Fringe*'s satire instantly recognisable. Moreover it was Christians who invented anti-semitism: "Though Pagans scoff and Jews deride"was one line from the Anglican Hymnal. The ignorant condescension with which gentiles sometimes treated their Jewish friends did not impress.

The two species of religion said to be growing most vigorously in the world today are, on the one hand, the terrifying fundamentalist wings of Judaism, Christianity, Islam and Hinduism; and on the other, Buddhism, which still advocates a "middle way". I answered Iris's question "Why Buddhism?" with intensity: "Because I have to do something about my mind." Buddhism alone seemed a species of practical mysticism that first explained altered states of consciousness, then showed how these might be used.

It did not bother me that religious manifestations of all kinds were attacked by some Darwinians. Do such spiritual techniques, they asked, provide any practical advantage in terms of survival? Advanced mathematical capacities – arguably – do not. Until relatively recently, no humans did any sums at all beyond the very simplest. Yet this huge capacity is there. Perhaps spiritual capacities are equally untapped. I didn't follow the feeble argument that Darwinism had rendered the spiritual out-of-date: Darwin complained in later editions of *The Origin of Species* that he found it impossible to stop people saying that he thought natural selection was the sole cause of evolutionary development, when in fact he had said only that it was the *main* cause. "Great", he said, "is the power of misrepresentation."

Religion cannot (by definition) be rationalised. A recent survey found that an astonishing 88 per cent of the British accounted themselves, in some sense, as "spiritual". Many of these were not members of any established religion.

I'm not clear why the image of Christ hanging, bleeding on a tree, a divine sacrifice, dismays me. Or why the wrathful deities of Tibetan Buddhism, by contrast, grimacing, bedecked with skulls, sometimes to be found in symbolic sexual union, strike a chord. They depict no "historical event" and are not "real". Even when borrowed from the Hindu pantheon, they are turned into aspects of psychic energy. They seem abstract, and meant to mirror the marriage of skilful-means-and-compassion; albeit sometimes alarmingly graphic too.

Much about Tibetan culture haunted me: for example, the Tibetans' traditional way of dealing with their dead. Neither cremation nor burial were common. Lacking many trees for burning as firewood and, for the long winter months, soil that can be dug, Tibetans practise "sky-burial" on sacred sites where bodies are broken up by professionals, the soft parts mixed with *tsampa* or barley and vultures and eagles summoned at an agreed point in the proceedings to descend and eat the prepared and bloody remains.

I dreamed about sky-burial, envisioning the impious Chinese tourists who, ignorant of its sacredness, flock to take photographs, bewildered when the Tibetan undertakers throw stones to deter them. Sky-burial seemed an emblem of uncompromising, direct communication with the grittiness of reality, its violence and terror. It awoke a sense of awe at our condition, a reminder that our world is sacred, and that all human beings, no matter how sophisticated, partake in a natural cycle.

Glimpsing the ox

MEDITATING

Fashionable post-modernism advises that the self is a flimsy construct, an illusion, a myth, a fiction. This the meditator discovers as experience, not theory. Life is a stream of becoming, a series of manifestations and extinctions, the concept of the individual ego a popular delusion. But post-modernity diagnoses our condition only to stop short of accurate treatment: few of the modish Western thinkers who argue that subjectivity is unreal, a potent illusion, a mere "junction for converging discourses", wish to put this piety to the test in meditation. We are also free (they imply) to remake ourselves in whichever way we choose, masters of our own destiny.

Back in South London I tried to meditate from a book, before finding an instructor nearby who could demonstrate how to meditate and, moreover, knew Chögyam Trungpa Rinpoché (the honorific "Rinpoché" – pronounced Rin-po-chay – means in Tibetan "Precious one"). Around 1980 she had helped lead a group of his students who – myself included – would soon move from a Balham terrace house to an elegant, spacious, beautifully converted Baptist Church – Shambhala Centre – behind Clapham High Street, where teachers spoke with impressive slowness and deliberation, un-frightened by the necessary silences during which accurate or eloquent thought gathers. The first gene-ration was partly hippie. Ten years later there were professionals: a professor of fine art, BBC producers, actors, a cancer-care specialist, teachers, aromathera-pists, many acupuncturists and computer-experts.

Patrick French, in his knowledgeable recent study *Tibet, Tibet*, gives an impressive list of reasons why he cannot entirely "buy" the Buddhist package: the schisms, bigots, frauds, hypocrites and predators that attend all religious systems; jet-setting lamas who prove (some of them) morally frail; inability to make a connection between meditative practice and the detailed horror of modern living; and, not least, the wackiness of many Western Buddhists, disenchanted with their own post-industrial culture, yet scarcely convincing, with their beads and bracelets, as representatives of an adoptive world. Of this, more later.

I was more fortunate. The Western Buddhists I met were concerned about the future of meditation in the West, and showed little interest in Tibet. They had discipline, a sense of humour and understanding, and were welcoming, on the look-out for new recruits but not importunate. They were little given to point-less Dharma-babble: to calvinistic denunciations of the ego-traces of others; to announcing, "You look familiar: *could we have met in a former life?*" They did not, unlike football manager Glen Hoddle, inform disabled persons that their "karma" was to blame*. Nor (shades of Communist Party-members pipe-dreaming the coming Revolution) prognosticate about enlightenment.

Trungpa's students offered a gradated path, and

---

*There is little in this book on 'karma' or 'reincarnation'. Karma, which is the law of moral cause and effect, is a fact of life and clearly a helpful description of our condition, but a hugely complex topic; as for reincarnation, while it seems to obtain for Tibetan lamas, I rather hope it doesn't extend to the rest of us – being born once seems to me a sufficient delight. Either way, these subjects are beyond my brief here.

favoured marathon meditation sessions. Probably few other sects or kinds of Buddhists put such emphasis on long sessions of sitting-practice. I now know that, for many, meditating for even twenty minutes each day is worth doing in itself. Athleticism is not the point. But I started strenuously. The first entire day soon felt irritating, impossible, astonishing, and then natural: the world slowed down, visible and strange. The extension of one's body in space, and of one's mind in time, seemed infinitely puzzling; and wonder, puzzlement and panic started to seem related ways of apprehending. It was possible to rest, to let go of complaint. I felt like the foolish woman who, having told the philosopher Carlyle that she now "accepted the universe", was answered, "*Gad! You'd better.*"

Chögyam Trungpa had been "discovered" in the early 1940s – a child to peasants who shared their surname (Mukpo) with the semi-legendary Tibetan warrior-hero Gesar of Ling – as eleventh incarnation (*tulku*) and heir to two ancient traditions in Kham, Eastern Tibet. He was educated by great Tibetan masters, including the head of one of the four lineages of Tibetan Buddhism, and grew up to be Abbot of a group of monasteries in Surmang.

When he was twenty the brutal Chinese oppression

started. China's claims to Tibetan territory are, to put it mildly, debatable, and doubtless influenced by both the mineral wealth and the strategic importance of the "roof of the world", from which China's enemy India might conveniently be threatened. Tibet's empty spaces must, moreover, have seemed tempting to a people living in overcrowded cities, while its intensely religious culture was inconvenient if not insulting to Chinese dialectical materialists.

Six thousand monasteries were accordingly destroyed; more than a million Tibetans tortured or murdered; nuns and monks forced at pain of death to "fly" from monastery roofs to show a gullible peasantry their lack of supernatural powers, or (it is claimed) publicly to copulate; numberless youngsters forcibly expatriated out of the "autonomous Region", indoctrinated and taught only Chinese. Then millions of Han Chinese settled in Tibet, where the once-peaceful landscape has been raped, missile silos placed, and many once-docile species hunted to the brink of extinction. The present King of tiny neighbouring Bhutan, the last Tibetan Buddhist realm on the planet, has proclaimed that "Gross National Happiness" matters as much or more than "Gross National Product". Tibet was permitted no such choice.

True: it is more prosperous than in 1959, but immeasurably impoverished and unhinged culturally. A railway and motorway from China will soon be completed, and the obliteration of Tibetan culture probably not long delayed; or what will amount to the same thing – its "preservation" in native reserves attracting tourist revenue, recalling the tribal reserves of drunken and demoralised native American Indians.

Iris called Tibet before its destruction by the Chinese "our last link with the ancient world" as well as a "corrupt", sometimes cruel theocracy. The entire culture has been construed, not wholly unjustly, as a conveyor-belt for the production of saints. There were once thousands of life-long retreatants in caves, crazy-wisdom yogins and yoginis (adepts, skilled in so-called "high" practices) wandering and preaching in outlying villages, scholars and Abbots who had completed a nineteen-year course of study, and – some of them – done cycles of three-year retreats to boot. With its more than 6,000 monasteries in which at least one in ten of its menfolk studied and practised, it was, for good and for ill, the most religious society on earth.

To the materialist it seemed a hopelessly antiquated system, with one class cunningly parasitising a superstitious majority. Even Trungpa is sometimes quoted as believing that this medieval culture showed signs, like pre-Reformation Catholicism, of decadence. Spiritual materialism abounded, practice had fallen into abeyance: the wealthy could pay for paupers to practise on their behalf. Many accumulated esoteric teachings without sense or understanding. Some Westerners do so now. The extreme view that Tibet was ripe for destruction is sometimes also voiced, Tibet's loss being the rest of the world's gain, the highway to enlightenment and the precious teachings on detachment, compassion and wisdom disseminated whither they were most painfully needed, in the dark and debased West. But how much better could this have happened without so appalling a toll of suffering, with Tibetan lamas travelling on Tibetan passports, and Western students freely making retreats in Tibet, enjoying its stupendous mountain landscapes, and studying unhindered in its monasteries.

Young Trungpa fled in 1959, like a million others, to India, a journey described in his autobiography *Born in Tibet*. After some years in Oxford studying comparative religion, he co-founded Samye Ling in Dumfriesshire, the first Tibetan monastery in the West; and was also the first Tibetan to gain a British passport. By 1970 he had shocked some by ceasing to be a monk, had married and emigrated to the USA where he founded one retreat-centre in Vermont, and another in the Rocky Mountains, the first accredited Buddhist University in the West (Naropa Institute in Boulder), as well as a monastery on Cape Breton (Gampo Abbey) and a centre in Halifax, Nova Scotia. He was colourful, a poet and friend of Allen Ginsberg, a horseman despite a stroke that left him part-paralysed – a legendary, powerful and controversial figure. His students compared him to the revered Padmasambhava who had brought Buddhism from India to pagan Tibet in the eighth century; so Trungpa Rinpoché had, one millennium later, helped bring precious Teachings to the West. A brilliant impresario and choreographer, he revivified ancient ritual and made its relevance to the lives of Westerners clear.

Around 1968 in Samye Ling, Trungpa gave students advanced meditation training consisting of the single-word instruction: "*Be!*". When they asked anxiously "How long should I *be* for?", they were advised, "Try half an hour a day." Soon they reported frustration: it seemed we Westerners did not know *how* to "be". Precisely this was our problem. A grounding followed, lasting many years, in the ancient technique called (in Sanskrit) "shamatha-vipashyana", meaning "calm-abiding, leading to awareness-insight". At first it resembles putting a protective glass sheath around a wildly guttering candle: once sheltered, the flame of awareness can start to burn more brightly.

You enter a Tibetan meditation-room with its exotic shrine and its precious silence and its practitioners seated well on their red cushions, surrounded by space and time, time and space. These were always there, but it was as if there had been no way to notice them, or perhaps it would have been too puzzling or threatening to do so. One calligraphy on the wall listed slogans: "Change your attitude and relax as it is"; "Work with the greater defilements first"; "Don't ponder others"; "Don't drive things to a painful point"; "Abandon all hope of fruition"; "Don't expect applause"; and more mysteriously "Don't give the ox's load to the cow."

Another (Trungpa Rinpoché's) read simply:

> Since all things are naked, clear
> And free from obscurations, there
> Is nothing to attain or realise.
> The everyday practice is simply to

> Develop a complete acceptance
> And opennness to all situations and emotions.
> And to all people – experiencing
> Everything totally without reservations and
> Blockages so that one never withdraws or centralises
> into oneself.

This "everyday practice" entailed meditation, and learning to meditate begins with simplifying posture. The best cushions are made of the hardest available foam – one foot by eight inches to sit on, and at least ten inches high off the ground; (three big telephone directories covered by a blanket also work). These minimize back-problems. A flat kapok-filled cushion under the feet avoids ankle-pain. Zen Buddhist practitioners in Japan might attempt lotos-posture: Tibetans generally don't. No self-punishment. Even in Tibet before religious expression was crushed, few meditated in more than half-lotus posture; but whether you are old or frail and need a chair, or fit enough to sit on a cushion, you start always with a straight back, fractionally straighter than feels entirely comfortable, with a bow-like curve in the lower back, and the sense of a thread pulling the centre of the head upwards. The head is in line with the spine. Eyes can be open, gaze relaxed and downwards, about two metres ahead. You learn to *occupy your spot*, it is said, like a monarch seated on the ground.

Good posture combines opposites. Strong at the back, vulnerable at the heart; relaxed yet awake. Vulnerability, which normally implies weakness, does not do so here, indeed it goes with strength. Likewise "relaxed" does not mean sleepy, but an alert passivity. Bodily pains resemble those accompanying first attempts to skate, ski, or ride. Muscles stretching, put to new work. Psychogenic pains, especially during the first full days of meditating, betoken resistance to letting go. Given time, they pass. Posture is expressive, even magical: indulging bad posture – a slouch or a slope – strengthens depression; so, conversely, adopting excellent posture in (or out of) meditation improves one's mood. In good posture the body sends the mind a message it may not otherwise be able to hear. You are said to develop "good head-and-shoulders", an attitude of mind as well as of body.

When asked how he recognised and distinguished his own thousands of students from other new-agers on Boulder's pedestrianised Mall, Trungpa Rinpoché answered, "They have good head-and-shoulders. And they don't bump into one another."

Posture somewhat established, meditation involves neither ascending to a higher state of being, nor entering a trance. The mind, normally "elsewhere" is trained to return "here". Allowing the mind honestly to meet itself and (later) what surrounds it, with less preconception. You work with returning to the breath, which can be counted. Watching the out-breath and returning to it again and again helps when you spot your mind straying.

Some say that they are *uniquely* unable to meditate, being too restless, too impatient, too physically unfit. But restless impatience, rightly understood, is less an impediment than a proper fuel. Hot boredom (restless, impatient, angry) is transmuted through meditation into cool boredom (patient, grounded, dispassionate), within which inner and outer space can eventually be discovered. What often gets in the way is the modern laziness that masquerades as busy-ness. We say "I cannot meditate" but spend hours *unconsciously* meditating, usually on ourselves.

In another sense "I" indeed cannot meditate: the person who meditates turns out to be new, and even unfamiliar. This meditator may even find more time to carry out other duties: some energy ordinarily locked up in apprehension and/or depression gets released.

Anyone and everyone can meditate and simplify existence – except the grossly disturbed, the border-line psychotic, who may be filtered out and invited to make tea or help in practical ways instead. D.H. Lawrence satirised a character whose thoughts uniquely cloud her head like flies. But we all resemble her. Thoughts arrive, for everyone, like the bitings of gad-fly; the training is not to scratch or inflame them, but let them be and pass: they quieten by themselves. It can seem that meditation "makes me" angry or lustful or whatever: the proper riposte is that meditation makes nothing happen at all except to slow one down so that one can witness how one always was, but never before quite saw.

"Doing nothing" is very hard work, like manual labour. The punch-line of an old joke has an Irishman, invited to explain how to get to Limerick answering, after some complex route-proposals, "Well, I wouldn't start from here if I were you." Meditating involves seeing that there is nowhere else to start from than wherever it is one finds oneself, and then seeing that that place was not so bad as one thought. "Fresh start" is what we claim to seek. Meditation provides the possibility of it, minute-by-minute. A new mind. It also discloses obstacles to new mind. To arrive (as T.S. Eliot put it) where you first started from but to know the place for the very first time, is the idea.

Sometimes meditation is accompanied by remorse at complicity with how the world is. And at the same time a painful sense of territory and self-clinging being consumed or going up, again and again, in flames. At the start we "cease being a nuisance to ourselves", the premise for stopping being a nuisance to others. At least, I used to think, I'm not harming anybody. And, even if my mind did not change, my back got slowly stronger and gave fewer problems. I had formerly spent a few days each year with a pulled back-muscle, lying on the floor and waiting slowly to be better. That mysteriously stopped, seemingly for good.

It can be shocking even to start to see how busy the mind is, constantly and inventively cooking things up. Most think we "know our own minds". Yet strange and hitherto unacknowledged thoughts approach like foreign armies marching over the brow of a hill, one after another. Thoughts can also have the speed of a water-fall, tumultuous, Niagara-like, seemingly unstoppable. Labelling all thoughts "thinking" helps, though difficult at first, so thick, fast and churning is one's discursiveness. Labelling helps most when done neutrally and non-evaluatively, but this instruction not to judge the thinking process is for some reason hard to remember, so deep is the tendency to see certain thoughts as "wicked", others as "good".

A common surprise for the meditator comes from seeing how many thoughts and emotions kidnap the thinker, taking him far away. *My thoughts seem to be thinking me*, instead of the other way round. Watching how automatic, involuntary, and repetitive one's thinking-processes are, it dawns on the meditator that "automatic, involuntary, and repetitive" are not bad descriptions of much human behaviour either, one's own not excluded. There is much cant in a liberal democracy about being left free-to-be-oneself. Meditation shows one's mind itself as un-free. Iris's novels have the same message: we are dark to ourselves, children in our understanding of ourselves.

This becomes painfully clear around those mental obstacles called in Sanskrit "kleshas", those thoughts – or emotions – which especially hold the meditator to ransom. A short list comprises: passion, aggression and ignorance. A simple experiment displays them. Standing in a busy corridor you watch the mind, which wishes to magnetise one passer-by (passion), repel another (aggression) and is indifferent to a third (ignorance). Kleshas cannot be transmuted before they have been noticed and felt. An instructive long gloomy list of kleshas includes *dogma* (not hard to see how that closes one off); and even "opinion".

The "accomplished" meditator would by contrast be someone less driven, shaped and blown about by each thought-wave, willing to take responsibility for states of mind, instead of (as in ordinary life) seeking somebody or something else to blame for them. Then the ability to respond to situations as they originate, rather than react to them in reflex fashion, might arise. The identical flow of experiences is the basis for suffering in the unenlightened man and for liberation in the saint. The latter has transmuted a fixed mind into a flexible one.

In China and Japan a traditional series of humorous cartoon-like pictures depicts the entire Buddhist path of self-transformation. These so-called 'ox-herding' drawings run like this:

1. A boy – i.e. an immature being – rope-in-hand, lost and confused, seeks his ox, which has escaped, is nowhere to be seen, and is out-of-control. This ox, here representing the habitual or stereotypical patterns of

behaviour which enslave the boy, is outside the field of his understanding.

2. The boy finds the first traces of the vanished ox, (neurotic mind, grossly disturbed or inappropriate behaviour) and starts his journey home.

3. The ox is sighted but elusive and declines to work for the boy, defying him: in a world in which he should be at home, his fragile mental economy can be plunged into neurotic anxiety, fear, hatred, depression and apathy.

4. The boy has lassoed the ox and tries to turn it around. He has to "break in" his karmic bondage and habitual self-pre-occupation. He forms the novel intent to reverse the runaway ox.

5. The ox has consented to belong to the boy, a significant reversal and the start of self-transformation, reshaping personality, motivation, through discipline, values and proper choice.

6. Boy rides ox while nonchalantly and confidently

playing a flute. The full force of the ox is at his command. Now both trusting and therefore ignoring it, he can give birth to playfulness.

7. Once again the ox is invisible, but this second phase of invisibility follows because it is trained or tamed, never rushing out-of-control. Self-forgetful and un-self-preoccupied, the boy can see the world. The sun floats in the sky and the boy enters Samadhi (meditative absorption).

8. An empty circle. Ecstacy, Nirvana, extinction of fear and hope.

9. Plum blossom, rock, bamboo, a gently flowing stream. Both ox and boy forgotten, the beauty of the world is all.

10. Laughing Buddha (also called: "Entering the market-place with Gift-bestowing hands").

At first you impersonate a meditator. "Everybody else in the room is probably doing the thing properly. I'm the only one counterfeiting… But – with luck – nobody can tell." Then, after a little while, some sympathetic magic happens despite yourself. By pretending, you discover to your surprise that you have been meditating anyway, without fully willing it.

Pop-existentialism told us in the mid-twentieth century to "*be here now*". This proves surprisingly hard. One's tendency is towards absence, distraction. Many thoughts seem like V.I.Ps, requiring a red carpet, special treatment. If certain thoughts seem addictive, de-toxing (deconditioning) is tough. One's discursiveness can also resemble channel-surfing, a ceaseless quest for entertainment and distraction. A movement of mind like a flea jumping is needed at first to start to train the mind to return to the body and the room and the present moment, and to learn to be without agenda. Doing less with the mind seems at first counter-natural. Relaxing is hard work: resting without strategy, or instant knowledge.

Not-knowing plays a role in Buddhism, a fuller account of which comes later. The original Buddha's mostly impromptu talks were in response to questions, some of which (fourteen "inexpressibles") he refused to answer as "non-conducive to enlightenment". These include: whether the universe had an origin or will have an end, whether or not it is finite, whether or not a

Buddha exists after death, whether or not the life-principle is identical with the body, and what is the exact nature of enlightenment.

He sensibly taught much more about the path to enlightenment than about the end-product. The question as to why we all have an ego if it is so unwholesome is addressed in the *Abidharma* teachings (which maintain that "we fall into ignorance") but still nags. One story records that the Buddha, on being pressed to explain the origins of the cosmos, "preserved a noble silence and passed on".

The Buddha compared the student seeking answers to all with a man struck by a poisoned arrow: before consenting to his life being saved by having the arrow killing him pulled out, he required first of all to know the exact name, address and village of the archer who had fatally wounded him. Many questionings, in other words, are fruitless. What Keats praised in Shakespeare as "negative capability" or wise agnosticism – the Cloud of Unknowing – sometimes serves best, and can start to give birth, it is said, to true insight, as lightning illuminates a darkened sky.

Comedy, humour, jokes come back. Not long after starting to meditate, I attended a big weekend with 50 participants. Many Tibetan temples have the gaudy *jam* colours a genetically modified bed-and-breakfast might exhibit if encouraged to spawn. This one in Clapham, like others founded by Trungpa, has by contrast a cool aesthetic restraint: he admired the calculated simplicity of Japanese taste. From an earlier incarnation as a ballet-school, there were mirrors along the back-wall, visible only to the time-keeper facing the assembled company, trying to sit in exemplary posture, and, every half-hour, gonging to start a session of slow walking meditation.

The mirrors provided the time-keeper with an alarming copy of himself, or, in this case, myself, since I had in secret fear volunteered for the post for three hours. I had a cold and didn't know I was allowed to move or blow my nose (I hadn't asked). An epic sweat-ridden panic-attack played itself out, heart kicking in fear, like a young rabbit trying to escape the chest-cavity. After a long epoch of rising hilarity someone in the front row facing got up, took out his handkerchief and, wiped my nose. I began to relax; comedy supervened.

Meditation started to resemble brushing one's teeth in the morning, a normal part of mental hygiene, that one will never get beyond. A few months of forgetfulness without meditating, and one's mind regresses at an alarming rate into all its old confusion. Meanwhile hearing teachings was like remembering something one tended to forget, again and again. "Ah yes: that's what it's like."

A French Catholic priest in his nineties was asked what, in seven decades of listening to confession, he had learnt about the human heart. Nothing, he at first replied. Then, having reflected, he vouchsafed, "There is one thing: fundamentally, *there are no grown-ups*."

Perhaps a meditator is someone wistful about the possibility of one day growing-up.

Catching the ox to turn it round

BASIC BUDDHISM

It is strange that humanist friends blame the religious for imperfection and self-righteous hypocrisy, as if to be religious were to claim to be perfect, when – from the inside – the spiritual impulse manifests itself firstly as a willingness to see that one is not. Religions often combine good with bad news. In Christianity, the bad news is sin, the good, redemption. Acknowledging one's complicity in the former is prerequisite for achieving the latter, and must presumably involve inner transformation and a re-seeing of one's world.

The meditator, analogously, is willing to find the good humour with which to encounter his or her own frailties, which can seem manifold. In Northern Buddhism (see

Chapter 5 – Positive Emptiness) the bad news is bewilderment or confusion rather than sin; the good is Bodhicitta or awakened heart – or Basic Goodness. This differs significantly from Western tradition.

Buddhism has no belief in Original Sin. Around 1984 an Irishwoman said to her Tibetan teacher, "What about guilt?" He replied: "I've heard of guilt. Can you just remind me what guilt is?" She answered, with wit: "It's feeling bad even about feeling good." In Northern Buddhism one's deepest nature is already pure, simple and good; what obscures it is an overlay, and one's considerable task as a Buddhist is to try to uncover something hidden and invaluable (the so-called "precious jewel"). I think this is more than a verbal point. There is in Buddhism original misperception (fixation-on-yourself-as-centre-of-the-universe), which leads to neurotic misdemeanours. Yet one is basically good.

It is sometimes said that Buddha is one of a series, each born to redeem a different aeon of time. The story of the most recent Buddha born 2,500 years ago seems both exotic, yet oddly familiar. It is oft-told, now even in Hollywood movies, some very bad. His name means the Awakened One.

Among the most influential figures of all time, he has

350 million followers today. The Buddha, a prince from (roughly) Nepal, was protected in childhood by his father from the ugly, violent and alarming facts of human existence; brought up in a pleasure-palace comparable to the world of television ads or a colour supplement – a world of perpetual prettified unreal youth, in denial of suffering and of death. "Human kind cannot bear very much reality": but he was in quest for what is real, and what is true. Escaping from the royal palace, he was shocked to meet an old man, a sick man, a corpse. Old age, sickness and death, he saw, were the common, inescapable fate.

This side of the story is still timely: like the Buddha's father, we hide sickness and death away in hospitals, attempting to ignore or deny their inevitability. It is curious that James Hilton's fictional Shangri-La in his 1933 novel *Lost Horizon*, set in a Tibetan Buddhist valley, resembles exactly the colour-supplement fantasy of unalloyed happiness and longevity that the Buddha was desperate to escape from.

In Hindu legend a god asks what the most mysterious thing about the world is. And answers that, although every single human being born on the planet has died, no single individual human being finds it easy to understand that this will happen to him too. Buddha left palace, position, wife and child to become a homeless wanderer, seeking understanding and release from the wheel of suffering. After trying out severe ascetic practices, he discovered the "middle way" and gained enlightenment in Bodhgaya, a town in North India.

The Buddha in his first teachings is seen as a doctor, prescribing a radical remedy for a defineable complaint, a raft to cross the river of suffering. His first sermon – the Fire Sermon (alluded to in *The Waste Land* by T.S. Eliot, who was briefly attracted to Buddhism) – concerned the Four Noble Truths: suffering, its cause, its cessation and the path to that cessation.

Unsatisfactoriness, impermanence, incompleteness, frustration, clinging, grasping and a fear of change are built into all. When one is invaded by the reality of suffering, seeing its all-pervasiveness, and feeling the pain of others (including unsympathetic others) the spiritual life, it seems, can begin. Iris, too, wrote "Man is a suffering animal, subject to ceaseless anxiety and pain and fear, subject to the rule of what the Buddhists call *dukha*, the endless unsatisfied anguish of a being who passionately desires only illusory goods." It is no accident that the Buddha first preached that the world is on fire with suffering. One's own suffering is the essential place to start.

Hearing this First Noble Truth proclaimed is oddly liberating. If on the one hand anxiety isolates, on the other, discovering Matthew Arnold's "turbid ebb and flow of human misery" to be the common fate is like re-joining the human race, finding community. When we become aware of the inescapable reality of pain we begin to feel fully alive, the opposite of gloomy: *seeing how things are* is a pre-requisite for happiness, even joy, since, from apprehending the mysterious transience of the world, its preciousness and sacredness become clearer too. Iris again: "Suffering is no scandal. All nature suffers. It suffers from being cut off from God, if for nothing else..." (*The Unicorn*). Understanding the First Noble Truth does not mean becoming fatalistic nor, for that matter, *laissez-faire* in politics. Neither the greatly admired, one-time Secretary-General of the United Nations U Thant nor his fellow-Burmese and fellow-Buddhist, the brave Opposition leader Aung Sang Su Chi, have proven apolitical or unwilling to fight for what was right.

The Second Noble Truth concerns the cause of suffering: belief in a solid, enduring "self" or soul.

Although Hinduism and Buddhism are shelved together as a single subject in Heathrow airport bookshops, the Buddha rejected Hindu belief in a soul: hence the Buddhist doctrine of an-atman or no soul. Buddhism is at odds here with Christianity, too, for that matter, with its doctrine of the resurrection-of-the-body or essential self.* For Buddhists the self is not a fixed or changeless product but a dynamic process always seeking an illusory resting-place where it might finally become "solid". The tramp-clowns who monologue in Beckett's *Waiting for Godot* are universal symbols, speaking for us all: the lonely individual struggling to talk into permanent existence, maintain and freeze something essentially fluid and contingent. Neither Godot nor a solid self will come to save us.

This self (ego) spends much time trying to establish personal territory, a nest or cocoon, to defend. It generally imagines itself as vulnerable, rather than

* This doctrine has always seemed to me pretty weird. I recall that, when I was (briefly) a medical student in the 1960s and studying anatomy, we were amazed to be advised to keep all tissues and body parts together, scrupulously, so that both relatives and God, on the day of Judgment, did not get confused by a Frankenstein collection of stray bits and pieces.

In the same spirit, W.E.Gladstone kept for 60 years his own finger-part, lost during a shoot and pickled in a jar, to be duly buried with him after his death, so that the Almighty, when the Resurrection came, should not find this crucial part of His creation missing.

robust. It files damage done to its vanity, and periodically audits the files. It re-heats the past, making "a mile out of an inch": a small perceived wound becomes cause for war. It is subject to incessant hope and fear. It goes on interesting forays into the future. It builds itself up and its main activity is daydreaming.

Ego constantly fears boredom and so cooks up entertainments and "obscurations" (kleshas) – passion, aggression, ignorance, which can also be seen as deformations of space, means by which we either foreshorten the distance between ourselves and others (passion) or extend it. Neurosis, unreality and confusion are not special subjects, but the ordinary human condition.

These first two Noble Truths describe the condition of Samsara, the *snake-pit* or *whirlpool* of ordinary consciousness, and it is our distaste or revulsion for this which brings us to the Path. If Buddhism is "escapist" it is precisely the discomfort of this egoistic anxiety that the practitioner longs to escape; and which may be worth transcending. The point is worth returning to.

One Tibetan chant accordingly speaks of the meditator as "not attached to food and wealth" and cutting "the ties to this life", indifferent to "honour and gain".

Reduction of Buddhism to this asceticism has led to its unfair reputation as gloomy. Tibetan or tantric Buddhism in practice does not undervalue pleasures, but it does warn and try to train against grasping and clinging to them.

The Third Noble Truth is cessation, respite, enlightenment. Nirvana has been conceived in various ways – a permanent bliss outside the conditioned elements of the world, a mind free from the illusion generated by desire, a realization of ultimate unity with the Absolute, a state of omniscience and compassion.

It is described most mysteriously as the extinction of a candle-flame, and, most comprehensibly, as a *cooling of the ego*. It is said that we glimpse this cooling through the "gap" that appears in meditation and shows our thinking to be other than wall-to-wall. When the mind exhausts its struggle with itself, a gap occurs. This gap appears to threaten our idea of ourselves as solid; or, from a different perspective, ventilates an otherwise stuffy room. Again and again thoughts bud, blossom, flower and die, in endless natural disjointed process.

People sometimes fear that enlightenment (or even meditation) might render its victims zombies, so that hospital wards would have to be specially dedicated to their treatment. The truth seems to be different: even a glimpse of egolessness releases energy, probably because of the anxiety-depression in which ego heavily invests. Take that away even a very little, and one can fly. Thus artists have found that meditation can unlock creativity – although not everyone's talent lies in going into three-year retreat.

The third Truth – cessation – precedes the fourth – the Truth of the path to the cessation of suffering, as if the practitioner might be encouraged by flashes of his destination long before arriving there. First of all the mind must (as Plato also wanted) be "turned around"; the method is the Noble Eight-fold Path. Right speech, right action and right livelihood (which constitute Shila or Morality); right effort, mindfulness, and concentration (constituting Samadhi or Meditation) and right understanding and resolve (Prajna or Wisdom).

The aspirant trains to behave gently and kindly; cultivating thoughts of loving-kindness is an antidote to ill-will. Practices of mindfulness and awareness lead to calm and to stability. Many world religions centre on sacrifice and on a God who may be bribed by prayer to rescue us. Buddhism centres on meditation instead. No one to save you except yourself.

Integrating such teachings takes time, energy, patience. In principle, one understands each successive stage first with one's head, later with one's heart, finally through what the *Book of Common Prayer* calls "inward digestion" so that teachings – ideally – become part of you and you no longer need to remember that you know them. The peace and alertness of the accomplished ones, manifesting Eliot's "condition of complete simplicity (costing not less than everything)", are said to be good to behold. Given that Tibetan teachers often spent two decades in study and completed many years in retreat, it is good that Westerners with busy lives and families are not over-ambitious; some, including friends of mine, have latterly completed the first three-year retreats.

***

Westerners, it seems, are specialists in guilt. When we find a way of putting down our burden, we sometimes use this new method to flagellate ourselves further. This is said to have shocked the Dalai Lama. Recently in Dharamsala he went round asking how many of the Westerners there used the Buddhist Teachings against themselves, "to increase their feeling of lack of self-worth"? On finding out that all in the room did so, he remarked, "Westerners really *are* different!" Trying to live in the present is difficult if you have no way of storing any good news about yourself. Life-beyond-hope-and-fear is all very well as a slogan, since from one point of view both hope and fear abstract you from what is happening now. Yet there is a good form of hope that is a virtue necessary to sensible living and planning too.

Egolessness does not imply lacking "a healthy sense of self". Indeed meditation requires this healthy self which, incidentally, psychotherapy can help build: there are overlaps between meditation and therapy. The possible ways an ailing soul might in any age be helped and cured is large: it seems the ancient Greeks at Epidavros thought that viewing drama was healing, and made it available to the infirm. These are intelligent partnerships.

Both Freud and Buddhism describe neurosis not as some specialised psychological perversity but as a natural tendency of the mind to distort, to create confusion. Perhaps this is why one Tibetan teacher told his students to "become ordinary" and so avoid the change from being regular neurotics into pretentious neurotics; another teacher put it like this: "You have to be somebody before you can be nobody." Spiritual practice could otherwise be used to avoid the need to face and work through humdrum psychological difficulties.

Another young Tibetan, asked recently why so many meditators appear to be "nutty", memorably replied that it is human beings in general who are disturbed. What those who meditate possess in addition is intelligence and courage: the intelligent honesty to see their own disturbance; then the courage to do something about it. Sometimes psychotherapy is an essential first step. Both therapy and meditation encourage a penetration of one's stories with relaxed and intelligent awareness. Therapy takes you into your tales about yourself; meditation does so too, but also encourages a gradual letting go of all stories.

So books suggesting that the Buddha and Freud saw entirely eye-to-eye generally locate their rapprochement in California, i.e. in Never-Never Land. Freud despised the religious urge as outmoded and prone to extremism, weirdly describing meditation in a famous letter as narcissistic gratification. Narcissism to a Freudian is characterised by the absence of any relationship with the outside world, and a belief in the omnipotence of thoughts. Self-absorption and primary narcissism are precisely what meditation cuts.

The paradox is that one starts meditating in order to change. Since we earnestly desire to differ from ourselves, *self-acceptance is change*. Change in the first instance shows itself in a willingness to stop taking one's spiritual pulse all the time, and in a willingness not to be in motion. Courage to be still. Then, at some point psychological impulses can be watched rising and falling within a much bigger space. We no longer have to act out every single one of them. Normally I believe my thoughts: what else am I but my mind? But the meditator starts to see that he is not identical to his thoughts, nor need he be limited by them. Strength comes therefrom. Mindfulness develops, and out of that, awareness.

Meditation proposes a way not of eradicating ego (too harsh) – but of ceasing to live exclusively from within the narrowing perspective ego offers. Discovering "Maitri"– unconditional friendliness, firstly towards oneself – is said to be an important preliminary stage on the path of developing compassion. Some, like the celebrated, bestselling North American writer and Buddhist nun Ane Pema Chödron, think it a later and more significant achievement: not everything is easily gradated. In either case, Maitri seems to help short-circuit one's internal warfare.

Discovering courage and "wind-horse" (i.e. good courageous energy) is interesting. I was brought up to believe that cowardice is fearfulness, and bravery freedom-from-fear. How else was the British Empire run? Meditation seemed astonishing because it indicated exactly the opposite. Cowardice for Buddhists is refusing to look at or acknowledge one's fear; courage is a willingness to see the shape of one's fearfulness *and then step inside it and act*, howsoever shakily, notwithstanding. Courage and confidence, it appears, might be developed by journeying inside fear. Fear is said to be the messenger telling one to "wake up": to panic is to mistake fear for the message itself.

How do people find courage to live and die? Virginia Woolf who, fearing madness, finally drowned herself in 1941 had earlier created in *To the Lighthouse* Mrs Ramsay, a character who contemplates the growing-up of her eight socially privileged children, pondering the pains of love and bereavement and work and work-lessness, and war, and dying that await them all. She feels life to be "terrible, hostile, and quick to pounce on you... There were the eternal problems: suffering; death; the poor... And yet she had said to all, 'You *shall* go through with it.'" This moving moment carries some of the book's truth, Mrs Ramsay perhaps symbolising an aspect of female life-force. In Buddhist terms her generosity is to transmit the precious gift of courage.

Tibetan Buddhism is foremost among the few Buddhisms that discuss, after much preparatory work, the direct transmuting of neurosis into enlightened energy. It speaks (perhaps optimistically) of enlightenment-in-one-life-time: even what is basest can be transmuted. This is said be dangerous. Its famous secret Vajrayana or tantric teachings propose a way of enfranchising all spiritual energy and transmuting it – just as, in the ancient dream of alchemists, base metal could be turned into gold.

Transmutation, which counts as a high teaching, is hard to describe, or accomplish. Heightening, intensifying, then stealing and exploiting the energy of an emotional obstacle, no matter how superficially "disturbed", is one description. Nothing is altogether to be rejected. "When we struggle against our energy we reject the source of wisdom. Anger without fixation is none other than clear-seeing wisdom. Pride without fixation is experienced as equanimity... Passion free of grasping is wisdom that sees all the angles." "The way up is the way down," as the Greek philosopher wrote.

Leading the ox onto the path

BUDDHISM GOES WEST

Buddhism, with its immutable truths about the human mind, has taken novel forms in each of its new territories. In its native India it had largely died out by the twelfth century, persecuted by Moslem and Hindu alike. Some early missionaries to Tibet, where by contrast it flourished, arrogantly assumed that its extraordinary iconography must necessarily be a corrupted form of Christianity. It is striking that the Buddha has been little known in the West until the last two centuries: Victorian Imperialists, researching the religions of the East in their original territory, declared the Buddha more congenial and "democratic", and less seemingly "pagan" than the Hindu pantheon.

Bringing Buddhism to a new culture has been compared to holding a flower close to a rock and hoping that it will grow. Sri Lanka, China, Japan, Tibet and the lands of Indo-China none the less each evolved a unique style and tradition, not always allied to state-power. In Tibet Buddhism allied, often happily, with existing folk-magic (shamanism) which sometimes challenged central Lhasa authority.

It is adapting again, now, to the needs of Westerners, by being at odds with the ethos of the age: materialistic egoism, individualism at any price, consumerism. That Westerners are taking to Buddhism is of interest to Asian Buddhists, some of whom, impressed by Western fashion, feel they have been given cause to re-value their own inheritance.

The millions born into Buddhism in the East, outside the caste of monks and priests, can be as incurious about what they inherit as the average Anglican. A Bhutanese friend travelled to France in 2001 to take part in a one-month Tibetan Buddhist retreat, and on the last day remarked on the irony that she had had to travel 4,000 miles to learn about her own birth-right. As a child in Bhutan she had had little religious instruction, and felt "four weeks old". What she encountered was not what she left behind. Such phenomena Christopher Isherwood lived long enough to applaud. In his novel *A Single Man* he celebrated the fact that a materially rich culture has a unique hunger for the spiritual. Poor monks in Asia might worry first about filling their stomachs and then about acquiring Rolex watches. Materially spoiled Westerners, he implied, were by contrast particularly ripe for teachings, being in a position to distinguish wants from needs. Having appealed to the first Western hippies, Buddhism now has a "yuppie" following that is differently disconnected and privileged.

Both groups played a part in creating California's renowned Zen Center founded by S. Z. Suzuki Roshi, author of *Zen Mind, Beginner's Mind* (unrelated to D. T. Suzuki). Its origins belong to the twentieth-century counter-culture, in which multinationals and the arms-race were seen as institutionalising delusion, greed and hatred, and "small" was "beautiful". Here on the West Coast one heir to Suzuki pioneered a show-case non-profit vegetarian restaurant (Green's) and a grocery store and bakery. These enterprises and some bestselling cookbooks (including *The Tassajara Bread Book*) helped fund Zen Center, which was befriended by the California governor Jerry Brown, and by distinguished poets and thinkers. Work-practice at the Center depended, contro-versially, on students taking only a stipend. This entire display of energy is happily remote from Japanese Zen which was latterly linked to militarism, nepotism, sexism and occasionally concerned with ethnic purity.

Zen practitioners in the West on the whole believe that they are perpetuating an ancient tradition. But there are also some wholly new and successful Western syntheses of different Buddhist traditions, such as Friends of the Western Buddhist Order (FWBO), which actively proclaim their novelty. And even those lineages in the West priding themselves on their "authenticity" have already made accommodations to their new situation. The whole idea of unlearning self-preoccupation, for example, has a very different resonance in a pre-modern society where ties of kinship, by contrast, are strong and sustaining. Here in the atomised and lonely societies of the West most practitioners have less support from family. And therefore un-learning self-preoccupation in the West is possibly all the more important.

Western Buddhism, it has been observed, begins by adding meditation and some exotic glamour to good works and a blameless life – without, it is to be hoped, entirely switching off one's intelligence. So many

American Jews and Unitarians have converted to Buddhism that they are nicknamed "Ju-Bus and U-Bus"; and one book is jokily entitled *The Jew in the Lotos*. Yet the flower is still tender, and further adaptations will surely be needed. One singular feature about Western Buddhists is their seriousness.

This does not necessarily refer to the absence of a sense-of-humour, but to the fact that lay practitioners, – especially following Zen and Tibetan Buddhisms, but in other traditions too – can be found who study and practise with the zeal expected formerly only of monks and nuns. In the old East a lay Buddhist might support a local monastery, and try to earn "merit" thereby, but would be unlikely to carry out months of retreat, or travel continents to collect teachings from meditation masters. Suzuki Roshi's biographer David Chadwick, himself many years a Zen monk, remarked in his Texan drawl of how some Westerners incessantly "shop" for new initiations and transmissions: "Too much religion [pause]… kinda *rots the brain*."

My first teacher Trungpa Rinpoché's style of teaching in the West was profoundly different from what he must have met with as a young monk in Kham in the 1940s and 1950s. Traditional Tibetan teaching as it still exists in many places is authoritarian, "top-down": the student a vessel waiting to be filled with ancient wisdom. Though a monk might be trained to carry out public debate, this has a limited number of known outcomes. Trungpa Rinpoché, by contrast, was willing to enter into dialogue with his students, to carry their scepticism and engage with their lives, setting a standard for others to emulate. It has been observed that: "He was the first Asian Buddhist teacher to plunge into the existential plight of a Western culture and to articulate a way out of that dilemma in the language of those undergoing it." His books have sold a million copies worldwide, and, since they are often based on public talks, sometimes include the original questions and answers of the students attending these. "Damn-fool questions" said Iris of the question-and-answers in *Cutting Through Spiritual Materialism,* though she liked it when, on being asked how he managed in the West without a teacher, Trungpa Rinpoché replied: "Situations are [now] my Guru".

Trungpa Rinpoché died after months of illness in April 1987, and his death precipitated one of the comedies of cultural misunderstanding that have attended the migration of Buddhism westwards. His remains were cremated in a big ceremony in Vermont attended by a large crowd, among them all the surviving high-ranking lamas of his lineages, seated in strict order of precedence, showing a preoccupation with hierarchy. Their presence betokened the great honour in which he was held. He had been given a high honorific Sanskrit title, meaning "tamer of beings".

During the weeks after his passing, and while this international event was being planned, some senior students read up on ancient Tibetan procedure. The death of your Guru is accounted an important teaching, from which blessings may accrue. In accord with ancient tradition, they salted his body in meditation posture to preserve it and, every few days, once the salt was discoloured by fluids leaching into it, changed the salt. This was exhausting and macabre. When they explained how they had proceeded to a venerable lama who had travelled far from within the Tibetan Autonomous Region to America, he – who presumably lived in Tibet in some simplicity – asked, wholly astonished, "But surely you know about deep freezers in the West ?"

Devotion to the Guru means having a singular unmediated connexion with the Teacher which can resemble falling-in-love or, perhaps, a psychotherapeutic "transference". This can be problematic – exactly as in psychotherapy – if an actual love-affair begins. Iris was upset that some described Trungpa accurately as openly having serial liaisons with female students. The answer that he was a Crazy Wisdom guru or "civilised shaman", wild but honest, failed to address her unease.

"Crazy Wisdom" is an ancient Tibetan tradition identifying wholly unconventional behaviour with progress on the Path. Among Trungpa's teachers was Khenpo Gangshar who took a female consort, renounced his vows, and became famous for eccentric behaviour, dying in the 1960s according to one story on his way to Beijing, having announced he would teach Dharma to Mao Zedong. The Crazy Wisdom teacher purportedly uses what might otherwise be seen as scandalous or unpredictable behaviour in order to wake his students up and – perhaps – free them from a small-minded judgmentalism. Thus though Gangshar's actions are described as embarrassing and disturbing, his words and actions are none the less seen as symptoms of realisation.

But the West lacks the tradition of "Crazy Wisdom". Here its appeal to a generation of flower-children and hippies has no doubt been different from its effect on Tibetan villagers. Iris talked of this for years. "I have committed many sins," she boasted, "but never that one"– having a liaison with a student. Clearly perturbed by the whole notion of Crazy Wisdom, she invited a Buddhist friend at All Souls, Oxford, to put me right on the matter, and later wrote to me of the hypothetical contingency of a document coming to light proving that the private life of Christ or the Buddha had been colourful – "this would not affect the truth of the mystical Christ or Buddha."

The historian Arnold Toynbee believed that the 21st century would see Buddhism and the West in collision. Perhaps he was right. Some such conflicts (analogous to those afflicting the Catholic church) recently became public property. In 1985 Jack Kornfield informally surveyed 54 Buddhist, Hindu and Jain teachers for an article in *Yoga Today*. He found only fifteen of the 54 teachers were celibate and 34 – more than 60 per cent – had had sexual encounters with their students: some in committed relationships, some casual. In 1983 Suzuki Roshi's heir Richard Baker was forced out of San Francisco Zen Center, which included the first Buddhist monastery established outside Asia in the 2,500-year history of the religion, because of sexual scandals and disagreements over his leadership style. (The story is told in Michael Downing's *Shoes outside the*

Door). The following year another Zen master, Maezumi Roshi, confessed to alcoholism and sexual involvement with a student. In 1991 Trungpa Rinpoché's American regent died of Aids after having infected one of his students. There was an inevitable sense of outrage and betrayal. Trungpa's son Sakyong Mipham Rinpoché did much to heal the wounds.

Around about the same time, it was widely reported that another lama, Sogyal, author of the bestselling *The Tibetan Book of Living and Dying* and friend to John Cleese, had been charged with sexual impropriety and that an anonymous donor had paid a large sum to avert a lawsuit.

Tibetans can be more relaxed than Westerners about sex – less prurient, puritan and hypocritical; sexual desire, feared and condemned in other religions – and in other kinds of Buddhism alike – is seen as the manifestation of an energy that can be harnessed for spiritual purposes.

"The sexuality of Tantra, real or imagined is not there for its own sake. It is a means to an end, although it is used because it is an appropriate means": you use a progressive series of methods, beginning by applying antidotes that remove some of desire's strength, then recognising its emptiness, finally transmuting it into wisdom.

This will not reassure everyone. Nor will the fact that consenting adults are involved. For if a student decides that spiritual obedience to her guru entails uncritical idealisation or even voluntary infantilisation, "consent" remains ambiguous.

Around 1990 the Dalai Lama, sensitive to public damage, helped an international conference on Buddhist ethics to address such issues and agree some public standards. He reassured anxious well-wishers that, "Buddhism is not new. It is more than 2,500 years old, and during that time such scandals have happened. But basic Buddhist teaching is truthful. It has its own weight, its own reasons, its own beauties, its own values." The wrong-doings of individuals cannot, he argued, affect the whole of Buddhism. He wrote moreover that, "Too much obedience, devotion and blind acceptance [i.e. on the part of the student] spoils a teacher." The resolution of that time of troubles has tended to result both in new, more democratic forms of governance in Western Buddhist communities, and in greater discipline and self-restraint.

Conditions of Western life make it impossible for teacher and student to work together as they did in Tibet: there a prospective teacher and student might spend years testing one another out before committing to work together. In the West, however – realm of poverty-mentality and impatience – such alliances can happen fast. Nor is it only Westerners who have problems today with devotion and deference. A most successful proselytising Japanese Buddhism, Nichiren-Shoshu, whose practitioners recite a version of the Lotus Sutra, has many million adherents world-wide. The movement is said to value and encourage material success. The rock singer Tina Turner is their best-known disciple; many actors and actresses have converted. For all the movement's success, however, its recent history has seen some difficulties: starting inside Japan itself, where the laity split from the monks into a separate organisation after disputes between the two in the 1980s.

It will take time for Western Buddhism to take root and for Buddhists here to be and feel unremarkable. In Bhutan and Buddhist South-East Asia you might be given at birth a "Refuge" name, and never give this name a second thought. In the West by contrast, to "take Refuge" – in the Three Jewels: Buddha ("Example"), Dharma ("Way") and Sangha ("Community") – is to make a positive statement of difference from your own culture, one compounded when – as can sometimes happen – the

Westerner elects henceforth to be known by his new Sanskrit or Refuge name.

For Hollywood, which has now started to pay Buddhism attention, and where Richard Gere is the Dalai Lama's best-known student, Buddhism has been equated to Tibet and its exiled leader. The Tibetan story was recently colonised in four films. Dsongsar Rinpoché's charming, low-budget *The Cup* shows what happens when a television-set is smuggled into a Tibetan monastery in India, to watch the world-cup. The best, Martin Scorsese's *Kundun*, a biography of the young Dalai Lama with music by Phillip Glass, was screened for a mysteriously short time. Chinese pressure on its makers (Disney corporation), and then distributors, was rumoured to be one cause.

Seven Years in Tibet, adapted from a well-known book by Heinrich Harrer, who is played in the film by Brad Pitt, overlooked the real Harrer's pro-Nazi sympathies. While the best-known, Bertolucci's weird *Little Buddha*, told the "true" story of the "discovery" of a young reincarnate lama in America, mixing this with a biography of the original Buddha.

Until recently reincarnate lamas were always Tibetan. Now it's open house. The occasional discovery of such lamas in the USA and of one in Southern Spain today is notable. But the "naming" of the action-movie hero Steven Seagal as a reincarnate lama is beyond my understanding.

Yet all this is scarcely the historical heart of Buddhism. *Little Buddha* nowhere points out that the *institution* of reincarnate lamas – "*tulku*" in Tibetan – was little known for the first 1,700 years after the death of the Buddha. It became important in the twelfth century at a moment when Tibetan religious controversy got mixed up with dynastic dispute. It seemed a convenient way of keeping precious Teachings alive: the belief was that the same few great teachers return, generation after generation. The very young reincarnate lama – as the film accurately suggested – once identified, could be brought up by senior monks who were custodians of the wisdom he must learn to manifest and transmit. This convenient arrangement appeared to guarantee the purity – and hence also the political survival – of a lineage, apparently freezing time.

The necessary interregnum between the death of one lama and the "proof" of his rebirth and enthronement, however, often made this a highly unstable system open to political manipulation by, among others, the Chinese who, if there were a proliferation of candidates, might attempt to co-opt the one most likely to serve their cause. Thus the Fifth Dalai Lama lamented that a simple hereditary father-to-son or mother-to-daughter system had not been generally adopted instead. (One sect, the Sakya Trinzin lineage, does something like this). The current Dalai Lama, best-known and best-loved of living incarnations, has on occasion criticised the *tulku*-system and mooted election for his own successor, if he has one. Certainly, election might have the advantage of minimising the risk of Chinese interference.

***

It is sometimes argued that in its Asian habitat Buddhism lacked – in comparison to the three great monotheisms – a socially engaged dimension. It is not uncommon to hear it said that the development of inner quiet among Buddhists should precede social action: the unripe practitioner can otherwise be compared to a Samaritan giving a man dying of thirst a glass of contaminated water.

The implication here is that inner purification matters at least as much if not more than public charity, or that outward altruism may hide inward aggression. And one does not need to have any interest in Buddhism to follow this logic or give it some credence: Dickens painted in his novels many such essentially comic hypocrites and impure public well-wishers.

Thus the great contemporary Vietnamese meditation master, Thich Nhat Hanh, is sometimes quoted as having argued that instead of saying, "Don't just sit there: do something," we should say the opposite: "Don't just do something: sit there." He added that learning to smile is "peace-work" and that the development of inner peace should indeed precede social action. The fact that such quietist pronouncements came in the immediate context of the violent hatreds generated by the Vietnam war is often overlooked.

This is, happily, not the whole story. If the world must wait until all have reached enlightenment before its problems are addressed, it will wait for ever. Sceptics indeed argue that two days of social service will do you more good than a week of meditation. But both together might be worth trying, too: during retreat your batteries charge, and afterwards you might feel you now have something to give away.

Thich Nhat Hanh has also argued that contemplation and action cannot and should not be divided. After he sheltered "boat people", published anti-war poetry, and defended those monks and nuns who burnt themselves alive in protest against the Vietnam War, a grenade was thrown into his office. A curtain saved his life. He was soon invited abroad, and both the North and the South of his country told him he would be arrested if he returned. He argues that "Meditation is a way of helping us stay in society" and of helping to make that society more liveable.

He is of course not the only great Buddhist teacher currently living in exile, his loss mourned in a home-country to which he is unable to return. When the Dalai Lama in his Nobel Peace Prize speech in 1989 affirmed that "Inner peace and happiness are the key" so that "external problems do not affect your deep sense of peace and tranquillity", he, like Thich Nhat Hanh, was scarcely proposing political passivity. One commentator has pointed out that both have had to deal with unimaginable suffering. Both are "examples of how meditative practice is the very ground upon which sane and loving engagement with the world is possible".

An International Network of Engaged Buddhists ("INEB": allied to the Buddhist Peace Fellowship in a movement known as "Socially Engaged Buddhism" and including many writers such as Gary Snyder and

Peter Matthiessen) campaigns on a range of social, environmental and political issues and would like to challenge consumerism. Monks in Cambodia and Sri Lanka have done much – and bravely – for peace and for the ecological movement alike. Glassman Roshi, a Western Zen Buddhist teacher in New York City who began working a decade or two ago with the homeless and with people with Aids, encouraged senior students to sleep rough in "street retreats", and started a community home-cum-gourmet bakery for purposes of rehabilitation. He began an innovative model project, Greyston Family Inn, training minority workers to remodel abandoned apartment buildings to live in. Trungpa Rinpoché's senior students helped.

More recently, Glassman has been running a famed annual week of retreat in Auschwitz; and training skilled mediators to work with victims of international disputes and help communication where this has for political reasons become blocked.

A San Francisco Zen Center student (Issan Dorsey), who came to meditation after a career as a female impersonator, prostitute and hippie, opened the Maitri Hospice for Aids next to a meditation centre, cut red tape, nursed patients, and was made Abbot before himself dying of Aids. A charity associated with Samye Ling in Scotland has helped feed and clothe the homeless in inner-city Glasgow, London, Barcelona and Brussels. Another, associated with FWBO, has helped ex-Untouchables raise their standard of living. A Buddhist Hospice Trust has created a network of people involved with work for the dying; and INEB's prison work has become enormous (Prison Dharma Network). Requests to the centre I attend for meditation practice have come from hospices and from prisons. Buddhism is not, as it is sometimes seen, "at best a harmless mystical preoccupation, at worst a socially irresponsible indulgence".

Sometimes engagement goes beyond reform to advocating some programme of radical social and political change, though precisely what social forms are being recommended can be hard to elicit. The Friends of the Western Buddhist Order have declared a wish to "turn the old society into the new". Trungpa Rinpoché founded a secular teaching ("Shambhala Training") on the premise that

> ...there is a basic human wisdom that can help to solve the world's problems. This wisdom does not belong to any one culture or religion, nor does it come only from

the West or the East. Rather it is a tradition of human warriorship that has existed in many cultures at many times throughout history.

The ladder of five separate weekends of meditation and teaching associated with this secular path is aimed at cultivating fearlessness and gentleness. It includes a variety of skilful means for arousing courage, speaks of realising the ideals of an "Enlightened Society", and is taught worldwide.

Riding the ox home

POSITIVE EMPTINESS

Meanwhile, and even if the alienated world cannot be called instantly to order, the mind can be called back to itself and, like troubled water, be allowed to settle and become calmer and clearer. Estrangement cannot be cured (and beware: the panics and other ills of the meditator can start to seem even more vivid); but the understanding of aloneness itself shifts and changes. The aim is for good aloneness, as opposed to the "loneliness of those who cannot bear to be alone". Perhaps self-estrangement can sometimes be helped by meditation which – like mountaineering – can transmute the fear of falling into a "rush" of courage.

In a bad panic the void seems the enemy and one

does not know or remember who or what one is. In meditation – by contrast – it could be said that one is learning slowly to relax into such not-knowing. This void or not-knowing here is, by contrast, not hostile. The panicker has hit upon something absolutely true and important: panics can come to seem like quasi-mystical experiences, albeit radically misunderstood.

The word "panic" comes from the Greek "pan". To be taken over by the God Pan – since "pan" means "all" – is to be invaded by the emptiness that has from the beginning of time secretly pervaded "everything", the heart-wish of mystics through the ages. For them the emptiness at the heart of the matter is experienced differently, even joyously. No-man's-land is where we always lived without knowing it.

Yet once you start to relax in meditation, fear can none the less arise. For the intellectually curious – and others might wish to skip this chapter – studying the various Buddhist views on Emptiness can help. Fear is said to be the messenger telling us to "Wake up"; if so, a panic attack involves fixating on this messenger rather than listening to the message.

Emptiness is familiar within our own Judeao-Christian tradition. The word "vanity" in "Vanity of vanities, all is vanity, sayeth the Preacher" (*Ecclesiastes*), one scholar (Northrop Frye) argues, could with equal justice be translated "emptiness": "Emptiness of emptiness, all is emptiness". Prospero in *The Tempest* tells us that we are "such stuff as dreams are made on; and our little life is rounded with a sleep"; and Psalm 90, as Shakespeare knew it, proclaims that: "We spend our years as a tale that is told."

Yet emptiness is not at the cutting-edge of our theology, and it may be asked whether we do not inherit a view of emptiness that is destructive, exemplified by that character of E. M. Forster's who discovered in the Marabar Caves that "everything exists: nothing has value."

When the first Buddhist Studies programme started at the University of Virginia 30 years ago, a jokey rubber-stamp was made and used on various objects, surfaces, and the foreheads of sleeping fellow-students. It bore the legend "*This does not inherently exist.*" Indeed Buddhism teaches much about "emptiness", and the witty historian of Buddhism Edward Conze notes that all Northern forms of Buddhism require of their students some preliminary emotional assent to the idea of "emptiness": the emptiness of others' fixations being always easier to see than our own. Suzuki Roshi: "True existence appears from emptiness. Our true existence comes from emptiness and goes back again into emptiness." One important recent text is entitled in translation *Progressive Stages of Meditation on Emptiness*. And, when Buddhism reached China around the first century A.D., the Emperor is said to have asked, "What is the first principle of Buddhism?" and been answered, "Vast emptiness".

"Who then am I speaking to?" asked the Emperor.

"I have no idea."

The idea of emptiness is so deeply inscribed in Buddhism that it can provoke both competitive debate and comedy. A recent symposium of many Buddhist denominations put on the same panel a venerable Korean Zen master and a wise, white-haired Tibetan. The Korean, a good deal of a showman, began proceedings by taking out from his costume an orange, which he carefully and slowly displayed to the audience. Then he turned to the Tibetan and asked, "*What is this?*" The Tibetan looked non-plussed. So the Japanese master repeated peremptorily "*What is this?*", expecting a learned disputation about the way the fruit combined appearance with emptiness. The Tibetan, who spoke no English, conferred *sotto voce* for a while with one of his monk-attendants, who was also his translator. After some minutes the translator said soothingly and apologetically to the Zen master, "Rinpoché wishes me to ask you: is this really *the first time* you've ever seen an orange?"

To be a devout Christian or Jew it is not required that one be a metaphysician. The same is not necessarily true of Tibetan Buddhists, who place great emphasis on the "view" or backdrop against which meditation takes place. A meditator without a "view" is said to resemble a man without either eyes or limbs attempting to scale a cliff. And such a view often involves a steadily deepening understanding of "emptiness".

P. G. Wodehouse invented a woman character, disappointed in love and with a clumsy desire to do good to others, who could empty any packed room within minutes. The teachings on emptiness seem designed first of all to make space within a busy mind for genuine compassion, and also to refine and purify that otherwise crudely do-gooding urge. Emptiness matters to Northern Buddhists because cultivating compassion is at the heart of their religion. When your own problems are acknowledged and start to seem smaller, those of others can sometimes be helped.

This is necessarily a gradual, and slow, process.

Indeed, Tibetans identify three separate Turnings of the Wheel of Dharma, three "views", each of which successively challenges and refines the previous one. These views work at two levels simultaneously – as a teaching of the Buddha, and as a deepening level of understanding that needs to be lived to be accomplished.

By analogy with Christianity: it is as if Protestants, instead of arguing that Catholicism is based upon "error", were to argue instead that God first revealed Catholic truths for the simple-minded, and invited all Christians to practise accordingly, before proceeding to the "higher" or "deeper" truths of Martin Luther.

As a way of dealing with doctrinal dispute this has much to recommend it: nothing and no one is rejected. No view is wholly wrong or misplaced. But some views are conceived of as belonging to the beginning meditator, others to the more advanced practitioner. One finds one's own level, and (in principle) should accomplish the simple before proceeding to the more profound.

The main doctrinal split in Buddhism separates its earlier Southern form (Theravada) in Sri Lanka and Indo-China from the later Northern form (Mahayana) in China, Japan, Bhutan and Tibet. An imaginary dialogue between a Sri Lankan Buddhist and a Tibetan Buddhist monk might run as follows. The Sri Lankan (a vegetarian who would not dream of touching alcohol) would say that Buddhism came earliest to his own country, and that the scriptures the Sri Lankans have inherited are the oldest and purest. He would argue that Tibetan Buddhism is a more recent synthesis of many foreign elements, some of which appear to the Sri Lankan heretical.

The Tibetan (who may eat meat and on occasion drink a beer-like potion made from barley) might answer that the question of which scriptures are earliest is complex. Tibet alone conserves Indian scriptures which, despite their arriving in his country more than half a millenium after Sri Lanka's conversion, are in their origins of very great antiquity and importance. He might ask whether the Sri Lankan system of Buddhism has produced a single enlightened practitioner over the last 500 years, and might claim that the Tibetan system has produced many.

Central to the Sri Lankan, and to Southern Buddhists generally, is the First Turning of the Wheel of Dharma, corresponding to the teachings, already discussed, on the Four Noble Truths. In these teachings on the Noble Truths Buddha discusses Emptiness as Egolessness or absence of fixation.

For Northern Buddhists, on the other hand, while these teachings are as precious and necessary as foundations are to a house, further teachings on compassion, on awoken heart, and a more radical view of emptiness matter also. Northerners somewhat patronisingly call Southern Buddhism by a term meaning the Narrow Way (Hinayana), as if Northerners alone have a monopoly on kindness.

In the South – so Northern propaganda maintains – you vow to reach liberation only for yourself. By contrast, an iconic figure for Northern Buddhists is Avelokiteshvara, the Bodhisattva of compassion: a Bodhisattva is an apprentice Buddha. On the point of enlightenment, he hears a rabbit screaming in a trap. He vows to keep returning until such time as all sentient beings might be freed from suffering. Northern Buddhists today take the same vow.

A debate beween old and successive new views about the nature of Emptiness ensued just after the time of Christ, each correcting increasingly subtle errors in its predecessor. Southern Buddhism had taught as part of the First Turning five centuries before that there are "atomic" particles of experience into which "ego" can be deconstructed. The Second Turning (c. 150 AD) corrected the view that such atoms exist irreducibly, and opposed their solidification. A philosopher called Nagarjuna, sometimes called the Second Buddha, was the key player. The *Oxford Companion to Philosophy* tells us that his teachings were therapeutically useful nonsense. They certainly cut all ground from under one's feet, rather as a Zen riddle or so-called *koan* does – e.g. "What is the sound of one hand clapping?" – and can accordingly provoke, deliberately threatening our conventional "fixed" view of ourselves and of our world.

This proliferation of views can be bewildering, provocative or downright irritating. While Southern Buddhists effectively discount the Second Turning (and indeed all later teachings), for Northern Buddhists the later Turnings are central.

In one key scripture from the Second Turning, for example, the Buddha also taught that there is "no suffering, no end of suffering, no cessation of suffering, no path, no wisdom, no attainment and no non-attainment". Here nothing at all has solidity or lasting substance. Pure generosity, so it is said, would be giving with three-fold purity : as if there were no donor, no gift, and no recipient. An act without trace. On hearing these teachings for the first time, some of the Buddha's senior students had heart-attacks and – presumably fearful of their own non-existence – died of shock.

Although some schism followed, monks of both views were none the less later recorded practising side-by-side within the same monastery; and Tibetan Buddhists today maintain that a grounding in the tenets of Southern Buddhism (discipline and renunciation) is the essential preparation for studying Mahayana later (compassion, skilful means).

This is not quite the end of the story. More recently teachings of the Third Turning point out the dangers of nihilism when "refutation" thrives without any positive assertion. If you take away all reference points, you might destroy the basis of the Path itself, and encourage a cold nihilism: the false view that nothing matters. To put the same difficult point another way: these later Teachings on Buddha-nature focus on the inexpressibly wonderful and luminous nature of non-conceptual reality. What the world is intrinsically empty of is merely the stain, confusion, neurosis which we bring to it, and which separates us from others, and from our world. Life is not an illusion (Hindu "Maya") but resembles one. Emptiness, properly understood, is not negation but, rather, openness. All beings have productive/dynamic Buddha-mind, which is living and creative. Even Nagarjuna wrote:

> Buddhas say emptiness
> Is relinquishing opinions.
> Believers in emptiness
> Are incurable.

In other words: "emptiness" is itself also empty.

Indeed "shu" within the Sanskrit word for emptiness (*shunyata*) – carries the connotation of being "pregnant with possibilities" – open – as well as empty. Beyond the protective survival mentality of "this" and "that", "I" and "other", lies an experience of the world's wealth "just as it is", empty of self-clinging.

Thus the encounter with "emptiness" is said to involve, properly speaking, not throwing everything out so that all that is left is a blank kind of nothing, but rather an experience of bursting into an openness that is rich, unbounded, powerful, creative.

While Europeans were murdering one another by the hundreds of thousands during the Reformation over (among other matters) whether the Communion bread and wine wholly – or only partly – turned into the body and blood of Christ, two Tibetans sects fought hard both for political dominance, and also over two opposing views of emptiness. At the time of the 5th Dalai Lama (1617-1682) some monks were forcibly re-converted, and texts from the new school were confiscated and hidden in the Potala palace in Lhasa, the wood-blocks not rescued for centuries.

To bring all this theorising and the seemingly endless abstruse disputes down to a practical day-to-day level and suggest its possible relevance in everyday life: recognising the emptiness of apparently solid thoughts of anger, pride, jealousy or desire when they arise slows down the chain-reaction process whereby they spawn further thoughts. Later, when you have gained some experience in the process of liberating thoughts, they are said to undo themselves as a snake might untie a knot in its own body. Finally, in a third stage, you master the liberation of thoughts, which can now, like a thief in an empty house, no longer cause harm.

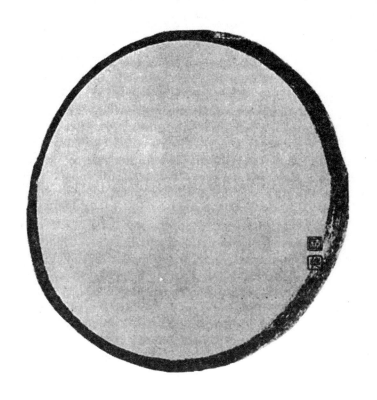

Boy and ox both forgotten

TALKING TO IRIS

Being with Iris was at first intimidating. Silences never fussed her, as they commonly do others. She listened hard, gave away little, and wanted always to learn about you, and your "life-myth": what made you "tick". There were few friends with whom she exchanged confidences about her own life, and one of these, who said he always began by getting her well-oiled beforehand, advised me to stand up to her. She differed with each friend, and gave each what she thought he or she required. It took some years to find in her the more open and animated friend I sought.

She had an excellent memory for the detail of one's life, helped on by her habit of slow, careful, spacious questioning. She gave the impression of living from shyness behind a protective carapace, having long since learnt to dissolve and let go of her own neediness through exploring the wants of others. I thought the underground themes of loving and being loved, and the difficulty of finding true reciprocity, ran through her 1982 Gifford lectures, under her great, sonorous, metaphysical themes (later published as *Metaphysics as a Guide to Morals*).

At Dino's restaurant where we usually met, she would sit and toy with her food and wait and watch and listen. Despite her partial deafness, she could hear here: the first floor was, apart from us, usually deserted.

Of course you knew you were conversing with a professional, prolific writer of fictions: friends would discover life-details they had vouchsafed re-appearing in her books, sea-changed. On one occasion in Dino's, having just learnt to stand on my head in a Yoga class and seeing no other diners or waiters about, I offered to demonstrate. She declined but put the incident into *The Good Apprentice*, when Meredith stands on his head for Stuart. On an earlier occasion we had supper, and I remarked on leaving, of the spiritual path and of writing, "It's a long apprenticeship"; and later wondered whether this helped prompt her choice of novel title. This was in her low-ceilinged, top-floor flat in South Kensington where her kitchen rivalled, for dirt and disorder, Tallis's in *A Fairly Honourable Defeat*.

Most friends were neither vain nor offended when such borrowings happened. One exception was the preposterously conceited and jealous Elias Canetti, the dark enchanter-guru who provided one model for her best power-driven demons, who haunted her work and my biography of her alike: Canetti's was, in December 1998, only weeks before her death, the last name she could be perceived to recognise. Although she would fiercely deny putting her friends into her work, this denial was at least in his case disingenuous.

Sometimes she surprised herself, as when hearing herself tell me in 1985, "Everything I have written is concerned in some sense with holiness." This thought, it appeared, was novel to her. The context was a discussion of the Tibetan Crazy Wisdom tradition, towards which she was hostile. She disliked discussing her fiction, and any observation about a novel of hers would fall into a deep hole, perhaps followed by, "Oh you mean something of mine." Then talk was steered back towards safety, which in our case often meant religion.

She was my teacher always. The mixed sense of space and of claustrophobia recorded by students in the presence of certain Tibetan Buddhist teachers was, when I met them later, already familiar to me from being with her. Goodness in her novels is not the ordinary human condition but always a special case, and it is a curiosity of her own life-myth that her good characters are always separated-off, and sometimes cold. A good man – she thought – would combine love and justice in his view of others. But her good characters often unintentionally make others feel more judged than cared for. This is as true of her first novel, *Under the Net*, where Jake feels – quite falsely – rebuked by the good Hugo, as it is in her later *The Sea, The Sea* where Charles feels admonished by his cousin James, though the latter secretly loves him.

When a director wished to turn *Under the Net* into a film around 1958, she proposed "simplifying" the book's philosophy by making it Buddhist. She had been reading about Buddhism since the 1940s, when she had planned in a novel (unpublished and lost) to incorporate the Dalai Lama.

Her interest flowered in one of her best novels, *The Sea, The Sea*, in which the hero James Arrowby is a Tibetan adept. The novel deserved the great acclaim and the Booker prize it won in 1978. Its narrator Charles Arrowby, a famous theatre director, has retired to live by the sea. "To repent of a life of egoism? Not exactly, yet something of the sort." He tries to escape his past but it returns to "get" him, as unfinished business. Having been rejected as an adolescent by the great love of his life, Hartley, and fearing any new pain-source, he has spent much of his adult life punishing his many mistresses with a memorable mixture of callousness and jealousy. A court of those he has enslaved assembles around his seaside retreat, acting as chorus to the main action. Hartley is living in the village, and Charles, never having recovered from her loss, lives out the consequences of his life-obsession in a tale that is comical, nightmarish, lyrical and reminiscent of Shakespeare's *The Tempest*. Charles is contrasted with his military and Buddhist cousin James, who can demonstrate what Charles finds hardest — learning to love unselfishly, non-possessively.

James is emotionally remote, which might seem odd, given that he is one of her "saints". The cool separated-off quality of her good characters reflects her own, as well as her picture of her own early good gurus.

This issue of goodness preoccupied her all her life. How achieve goodness? And then how — as a novelist —

depict it? Her work is at odds with Western self-centred individualism. Man, she wrote, is a creature who creates pictures of himself and then comes to resemble the picture. The view her philosophy gives of the psyche is one a Buddhist would have no difficulties with.

Her seminal *The Sovereignty of Good*, published in 1970, enlivened a bad summer (she replied to my fan-letter written from an Unthank Road address thanking me for "so cheerfully belying my address"). This book is rightly Iris's best-known work of philosophy. Its influence has grown since it was first published. It was fiercely original, a passionately argued attack on both Anglo-Saxon and French orthodoxies, the fruit of a thorough professional involvement with the school of thought to which it was opposed. It was said to have returned moral philosophy "to the people", those "not corrupted"[*sic*] by academic philosophy: lay readers gained illumination from it, as well as philosophers. It was a call to action, a programme for human change by the lonely individual. It located value within attention to good things in this life, as well as in the spiritual quest. It also lucidly proposed a powerful and interesting "rival soul-picture" which shares something with Buddhism.

The psyche is, she argued, a historically determined

individual relentlessly looking after itself: mechanical, hence unfree, and given to daydreaming. Reluctant to face unpleasant realities, the mind is not normally a transparent glass, but a cloud of more or less fantastic reverie designed to protect from pain. It constantly seeks consolation, either through imagined inflation of self or through fictions of a theological nature. "Even its loving is more often than not an assertion of self." She wrote that we can "probably recognise ourselves in this rather depressing picture".

She provoked by being brave enough to challenge modern pieties, connecting goodness not with finding a fixed identity, but with letting go of exactly that vain quest. "It did not matter having no identity," a wise character in *Nuns and Soldiers* assures a younger friend. Her novel *Bruno's Dream* ends with Diana nursing the dying Bruno while contemplating movingly, "She tried to think about herself but there seemed to be nothing there... One isn't anything, and yet one loves people. How could that be?" The same note recurs throughout: we don't exist all that much. *The Black Prince* asserts that, "We are tissues and tissues of different personae, and yet we are nothing at all." People rarely think genuinely about one another in her work but invent fantasms which they deck out for their own private purposes.

Iris feared that belief in goodness might disappear now, together with God and the afterlife. Her own goodness is clear in her very many and wide and dispassionate friendships – "I love you ever so much, and send ever so much love," she wrote in the autumn of 1994 – and in her generosity in encouraging other writers, whose work, when invited, she always read with an unfailing generosity of spirit and a close attention to detail: rare qualities indeed in a writer vis-à-vis her peers. A passionate stilled attention – "watching as a dog watches" – was her path, recalling the highest teachings of Tibetan Buddhism, which put the greatest possible premium on mindfulness and awareness.

The view she advanced in her 1982 Gifford lectures, that a virtuous apprehension of others has its roots in sublimated sexuality is one that would not have astonished the Plato of the two "erotic dialogues" – *Phaedrus* and *Symposium*. A Tibetan Buddhist would be quite at home here also. The transmutation of passion into compassion is fundamental to all three: Plato, Iris and the Tibetan.

One of her characters remarks that there are friendships in which you discuss religion, and others where you talk about love (*Bruno's Dream*). We started with religion. She wanted to know whether a human being can change and, if so, how this might be done; and whether even a small change might have large consequences. I kept her letters and drafts of a few of mine to her.

In May 1983 she wrote thanking me and my partner Jim O'Neill, "I absolutely loved being with you both... and felt entirely at home with [Jim] at once." In June that year she commended John Blofield's *The Way of Power*, which I believe had been a source for her when researching *The Sea, The Sea*. It had, she wrote "a lot of good things, as well as much picturesque information." Blofield had evidently mentioned Samye Ling, the Buddhist monastery Trungpa co-founded in 1969 near Eskdalemuir in Dumfriesshire. We went there as a result of the letter and listened to a talk on karma and watched resident-practitioners spin honey-combs in a centrifugal machine to make honey.

By 1985 I started sending her all Trungpa Rinpoché's then-published books. "I will report on [him]," she advised. Later that year, "I wish I could sit with you! You are a dear good boy now, & will be even more so when you achieve enlightenment!"

Early in 1986 I wrote to describe my first (and only) meetings with Trungpa Rinpoché, who gave a public talk at the Friends' Meeting House on Euston Rd. I had never before seen him and thought he looked small, old and grey. I reported his talk as "not good. Those with a strong connexion thought he was acting out [the message of] 'no reference point'; an Oxford theologian who was with us thought it was flu, but in fact it was saké."

The following Friday he came to our centre in Clapham and looked, instead, unaccountably young and golden. "He is passionately Anglophile, partly because of the good time he had as a Spaulding Fellow reading philosophy in Oxford in the 1960s; he thinks we have kept the 'warrior tradition', kin to Buddhism, intact." By this tradition he meant an unusual and perhaps paradoxical blending of gentleness and fearlessness.

I was one of those serving him shakily in the Balham house where he stayed, and I cooked dinner for him — roast lamb and potatoes, carrots glazed in sugar and butter. Like many Tibetans from the high plateaux, he liked fatty foods.

A high premium is put on devotion to the teacher, and, prior to Trungpa Rinpoché's visit, we had spent hours redecorating the house and refurbishing. The atmosphere, I wrote to Iris, resembled an Oriental court:

We minions were in the kitchen; and there could be a dozen or so people there… with so many people and so many nationalities and so much desire to please there was a good deal of tension, & one learnt from swimming in that. I liked the style of us English best – not as efficient as the Dutch or Germans but more jokes, kindness and good humour… Over all I felt, again, that meditation is a good thing, helping make people a very little more open, kind, patient, calm, though there can be no guarantee that the energy it releases is used properly; when I doubt, a brief look at those who don't meditate reminds me that if we are usually dotty, they are often very mad indeed!

That he was accompanied by a female "consort" worried Iris but not me: there was a total openness and absence of disguise. "One weird and fascinating and perhaps instructive thing about Tibetans has been their cheerful indulgence of worldly frailties in their great Teachers, and their extraordinary ability to combine this + absolute devotion… I sometimes wonder if there is a lesson here for puritan Westerners such as me [*I meant, of course, Iris herself, also*]: and whether this is connected to a cheerful tolerance? Marpa (Milarepa's teacher) had a horrible temper and beat his wife..." I mentioned that the journey described in Trungpa's Shambhala training teachings – from the "cocoon" of the ego towards the vastness of "Great Eastern Sun" vision – sounded like Plato's "great myth" of the Cave and the Sun from *The Republic*, a myth she loved and made much of. (This envisages the mass of humankind as slaves trapped in a dark cave, fooled and alarmed by the shadows that they watch, cast upon the walls.) She replied, "I'm all for leaving the cocoon & making for the Great Eastern Sun, but not so sure of my ability for cheerful tolerance. (That problem worth reflection of course)."

In 1988 I prepared to spend eleven weeks in a group retreat in tents high in the Colorado Rockies. This was the then long customary preamble to receiving permission to start the "secret" Vajrayana teachings peculiar to Tibetans. One took, I believed, a vow of loyalty to the whole enterprise "the consequences of breaking which, after so many weeks of meditation, are sickness, or worse".

Iris worried: "You must keep in mind that the aim is

supreme goodness, not supreme power! However you are already experienced and wise and will know what to do." Soon she wrote again, "I feel inclined to make a sign of the cross over you. But will not suggest that you wear a crucifix... your part of the Rockies might be rather full of ambiguous electricity – but you will walk unscathed among demons without such extra aids."

I wrote on arrival:

The setting is superb. Alpine meadowland at 8,000 feet bounded by pine-clad needle-like peaks an C18th Chinese master would have loved to paint. Amazing variety of plants, some recognisable (briar-rose, yarrow, wild iris, marigold, true geranium, harebell) and animals which – as in pre-1959 Tibet – show, after 15 years of Buddhist habitation, little fear of us. Deer, rabbit and ground-squirrel come right up to our tent, chipmunk enter it at night for biscuits. Rabbits joined in the circle of an open-air discussion for five minutes, frolicking, and mice have nested in and shredded my new sweaters... The weather is as capricious as one's mind – 90 by midday, near freezing at night. It... often hails, rains most days and there are frequent showy electric storms.

The tent I shared with a kind Texan was flooded the first day, and some days later too. You could walk up for an hour and see the snowy continental divide itself. West of this all rain finds its way into the Pacific; east of it water debouches into the Atlantic. It was an extraordinary luxury to have three months off in the middle years, a measurable fraction of a whole life-time. Time was visible here. There were the last winter snows on arrival in June, and then the first of the new ones on departure in September. Migrant barn-swallows arrived. You watched them nest in practice tents, hatch and feed their young, which then fledged and learnt to fly and finally left for Mexico. A small placard near the meditation-tent bore the optimistic legend, "Good and bad, happy and sad: all thoughts vanish into emptiness like a cloud in the sky." Not all thoughts disappeared at the same speed.

"Our schedule is a traditional Tibetan one," I continued, "with our three months divided into three 'Yanas' or paths. First month was Hinayana (= strict way) which had a rat-in-a-trap... lonely feel to it; now we're in Mahayana (= open way) concerned with awakened heart &tc; from July 30 comes Vajrayana (= way of transformation), the much discussed secret Path.

So there are transitions... Meals are Zen style, on the floor, and Precepts are taken (no killing, theft, untruth, sex, alcohol)." In fact the first three precepts were embraced enthusiastically; the last two (renouncing sex and alcohol) only by a minority. Many fell in love. Everyone had three daily hours of menial tasks and I wrote to Iris truthfully that "I admire and like the kitchen crew best": they were daily feeding over 400 people, 150 staff, 250 participants, one third European, the rest North American. There was even a school for 50 children. "One misses home like mad." It was lonely. There was no landline out and – this was the pre-mobile epoch – telephoning was complex and pricey, involving a satellite dish. I cheered myself up by putting out a special 1-to-4 sugar-in-water mix hung within a cup outside our tent, to invite humming-birds, which duly arrived, tiny red-tailed, green-backed samurai in iridescent armour – zipping around like bees on speed – duelling non-stop with each other like fighter-pilots and feeding.

Iris replied, "I like to hear of the tame animals and birds enjoying the spiritual atmosphere. And so it was thus in Tibet in the old days." She was interested that outsiders could visit. It was not a closed environment. There was one tent with two *tulkus* or reincarnate lamas about whom she requested further intelligence; but they were young and played cards and had fun and there was little to report. "I feel the greatest curiosity, likely to be unrewarded, about the secret teachings!"

I had written to her, as well as of good times, of raw and rugged and vivid panics: "animal frights, anxieties, sometimes a horror at not knowing what it is one is". "What I can I think a little imagine", she replied, "is your not-knowing-what-one-is-feeling. I feel this may be, in that context, a 'good thing'. After all, what *is* one?" She noted that I admired the kitchen staff best but wanted to know "how much this scene depends on veneration of certain obviously holy figures (I mean real present people)... where is 'good' in all this?".

I replied that I loved the richness, profundity and vastness of the teachings, and the way they combined, "a 'mystical' path with the most intensely earthy practicality and good-humoured, cheerful realism". But since the main teacher of the seminary was sick and absent, there was little I could tell her about him. Teaching seemed to me in any case a skill many could acquire: cooking three meals a day in simple conditions for 400 required constant patience, skilful means, energy and compassion. I genuinely admired the kitchen heads. And, though I shared some of her scepticism, it increasingly seemed that she perhaps made too much of "Good" persons. We are all made from the same frail/ poor stuff and a Buddhist who fully knows this might be described as "skilful", as "accomplished", even as "realised", implying some accumulation of merit and insight. The Tibetans wrote little of goodness *per se* but rather advocated an increase of compassion, and, above all, of skilful means i.e. learning to work appropriately with whatever is happening right now. This seemed more practical and helpful than Iris's absolutism.

Iris variously called "ego" in her philosophy "raging", "greedy", "fat", "relentless" and given to "rat-runs" of fantasy. Indeed later, troubled by her fetishism of the Good, I wrote suggesting that the word Good be de-commissioned, or spelt only as the Orthodox write the name of the Almighty, without vowels: "G**d", a name not idly to be said, lest it sound blasphemous or priggish.

We differed, also, about magic, a topic in which Irish Protestants like Iris have long shown interest. In *The Sea, The Sea*, the paranormal plays a picturesque role. The egotistical theatre director Charles Arrowby asks his good cousin James – the Buddhist adept – about an Asian he once sighted in James's flat. "Oh that was just a tulpa,"

James enigmatically replies. Iris explained that "tulpa" comes from Alexandra David-Neel, "I forget which book (*Mystics, Magicians in Tibet?*)" meaning another being brought about by mental concentration. "(So not necessarily good – though perhaps intended [for] good purposes?)… an ambiguous project anyway!" David-Neel tells how the tulpa she created to help her in religious work ate all the camp food for six months, was generally tiresome, and it took trouble to find the right spell to de-materialise him. "I am glad you will not be bringing one of *those* back with you from Colorado!" Iris wrote.

David-Neel, I replied, sensationalised Tibetan religion: she was overly interested in the paranormal, which, if it exists, does so merely as an unimportant (if colourful) by-product of the spiritual quest. The paranormal interested Blofield too, who in turn influenced Iris. His foot-noted account of levitation gets into *The Sea, The Sea* when James rescues Charles from drowning in a steep and smooth-sided pool. James also practises the yoga of inner heat – the well-attested ability of adepts to raise body-temperature – useful in a cold climate.

These things mystified me. True, in Northern

Buddhism the Buddha himself is closer to being a supernatural figure who can help us. And one part of the quality of Buddhas and Bodhisattvas is their mysterious ability to calm us down and cheer us up, so that we put down our burden. Yet Milarepa, like Teresa of Avila, whose pockets were filled with stones to hold her on the ground, tended habitually to like also to levitate and fly. Why, on the wish-list for Universal Saints, do they check off air-miles, rather than the ability to quell flood, famine and war? As the Dalai Lama has put the matter, "the real miracle of Buddhism is how a person can change, from a very empty person to a person who is full of compassion".

But Tibetans hold many uncanny beliefs: for example, that one can expel consciousness at the time of death – also part of the apparatus of *The Sea, The Sea* – or learn "lucid dreaming" – the ability consciously to guide a dream. Iris's journals show that, untutored, she had exactly this latter gift herself: the frontier between unconscious and conscious energy is less rigidly patrolled in an artist than in the rest of us.

One "Old School" tradition maintains that the enlightened can attain Rainbow Body, whereby, after having been locked in a state of meditative absorption for days, they physically disappear, leaving only their fingernails, toenails and hair as marks that they were ever with us. A Tibetan lama-friend thought Alec Guinness's rapid disappearance as Obi-Wan Kenobi in *Star-Wars* recalled Rainbow Body.

When I asked Iris about her own sense of the word "magic", she replied, memorably and helpfully, "I think it's everywhere just over a certain borderline – where a kind of will-to-power radiation takes possession of up-till-then innocent or harmless or spiritual images… activities… or states of being". Renunciation of the will-to-power is the theme of *The Sea, The Sea* as well as the leitmotiv of Iris's own life-search.

Lest my own approach sound overly rationalistic or sceptical, a strange tale follows. In May 1987 I attended the cremation of Chögyam Trungpa on a day of heavy mist near a small town in Vermont. At the moment the funeral pyre was torched, parting clouds revealed in a clear sky two concentric, complete rainbow circles around the sun. Iris conferred about a photograph I took of this with her friend the comic writer Honor Tracey, who, putting on her occasional County Mayo brogue, announced reassuringly, "Sure concentric rainbows around the sun happen all the time on the West coast of

Ireland." Unexplained rainbows also figure in Trungpa's autobiography *Born in Tibet*.

After these rainbows, three eagles – or possibly red-tailed hawks – flew in *stage right*, circling the pyre before departing; following which strange and multi-coloured clouds, golden or turquoise, appeared in the sky, suggestive to some of symbols. Sceptical journalists from e.g. *Time*, *Newsweek* and the *New York Times* were bemused, some suggesting implausibly that lamas might surreptitiously have fed the fire appropriate chemicals. I had no explanation. To be among the crowd of 3,000, applauding, wanting more, was moving.

Iris could not understand the fact that Tibetans "visualise" in deity-practice, and that the visualisation might be female – "Not like meditation on Christ's passion. Seems dangerous... interesting about the female deity. The sex of one's god must be a very deep matter. I think my daemons are all male." I tried to reassure her by being down-to-earth, and praising the group-intelligence in which one can feel oneself mirrored within a Sangha or community: "I feel I've been taught a lot of truth by fellow-Buddhists." ("At least you'll make new friends," she remarked good-humouredly).

She came for dinner on my return from Colorado, to

witness any effects, and declared me later as "so glowing with being". Indeed I felt newly-hatched, and less alarmed by her. She also wanted to meet our blue-eyed collie, Cloudy ("I should like to meet that Beast") who appeared five years later as the dog Anax in *The Green Knight*.

"What a happy utterly special dog… so beautiful and so strange. Well that applies to you, too, mutatis mutandis." Soon "I hope you have more writing plans, which will… live in mutual harmony with your spiritual life… I wish I could talk to you more and learn a thing or two."

She twice spoke of my teaching her to meditate, but out of mutual shyness we did not proceed: she had, in any case, had meditation instruction before. "As for Buddhism, I understand little – nothing," but foot-noted this, "I mean in a sense of a sense [*sic*] in which it doesn't altogether matter. Perhaps this is a Buddhist thought"… "I certainly don't think Christ is to save us/everyone. I guess that Buddha will save more… I have learnt more from Buddhism." But she wished she understood more: "You are really inside."

I joked once that I identified happily with the religious fools of her novels. She rebutted the identification with the optimism of a kindly aunt: "You are wise and holy... I see you... upon a high track." Her letters sometimes request elucidation: "Please tell me more about Shunyata [emptiness] and is it a good thing to be driven through that narrow funnel?" She hoped there would be more of "us" "to save the next century".

In 1984 she had written hoping we would in Radnorshire acquire "those 3 acres & brook" – we did buy them – where she would spend much of her last three years. "Be well, be happy," her 1995 Christmas card read. The following June she and John Bayley came to stay in Radnorshire for what turned out to be the first of very many weeks. Over her last three years we became like family, and had to learn the skills involved in caring for someone with Alzheimers.

She taught me in her prime: then, much later, she taught me differently in her decline. Although sometimes terrifying to watch it was also infinitely moving to see with how much gentleness and courage she relinquished her own identity.

A Buddhist lesson here, perhaps. It was a challenge to write her *Life*, which had its own share of emotional chaos, without belying what both Buddhism, and also Iris, had taught me: refusing glib knowingness, and with the generous kindness she unfailingly manifested.

Charting her journey from brilliant bohemian youth towards the wise serenity, celebrated in Tom Phillips's iconic portrait of her in the National Portrait Gallery, was taxing. It did not seem strange that a bohemian could become a sage: how else is wisdom born, if not from contemplating one's frailties? The Phillips portrait is a truthful one. But I believed (rightly, as it turned out) that the secular ethos of the day might have difficulties with the idea that her life , or any life, could manifest a slow, deep change.

I could not have found the courage to proceed without the little learnt from meditation, and owe her gratitude for that, too. If we had not met in 1982, I should in all likelihood never have discovered Buddhism. When she died in 1999 she left me in her will a beautiful Gandhara stone head of the Buddha, whose enigmatic smile lightens our kitchen.

The beauty of the world is all

STORIES

All "stories" are problematic. And there is something odd, perhaps fake, about making the meditative path into a "story". Iris's first novel has a hero who knows, too, that all stories are lies. A later novel again asserts that "the spiritual life... has no story" (*The Unicorn*). Yet we value novels because of their stories: only through stories can we get at the truth.

The spiritual life has no story because it has no hero; and meditation, while someone must perform it, has in some sense no subject. *Thoughts without a Thinker* is the title of one book on the topic. Meditators will thus say that they have been "sitting" or "practising" rather than "meditating".

Shedding one's biography, or skin, is one point of meditation, which, if this can be begun at all, can only happen through a journey down into all the contradictory "stuff" from which one appears to be made, where Yeats taught us that all ladders start: "In the foul rag-and-bone shop of the heart."

One of the greatest living Tibetan meditation masters – Khenpo Tsultrim Gyatso – is often compared to the "Lord of Yogis Milarepa", whom he resembles in both substance and style, and whose songs he has taught from. He has no fixed abode, few possessions, has practised for years in solitude, sometimes sealed in darkness.

He was on meditation retreat, perhaps for life, in a cave in Eastern Tibet when alerted to Chinese violence in 1959, and unwillingly broke his retreat to flee to India with a group of nuns whom he took under his wing. He was once asked by his students to tell them a story about the many three-year retreats he is believed by then already to have completed. He recounted, in two sentences, the happiness he once felt, watching the sun come up.

***

After a honeymoon period when the new meditator is in love with practice, it usually becomes clear that "going

Buddhist" is neither a quick fix, nor a one-shot deal. Those who believe that it takes many life-times to perfect oneself can find necessary patience in the idea of reincarnation. (Though one writer-friend says it seems an unpleasant trick: "Just when you think you've got through with the business of living and dying, they recycle you as an earthworm.")

In the meantime, a willingness both to see through your stories and to meet repeated disappointment is sometimes said to be the best way to proceed. Some get discouraged by the sheer demandingness of this – the long hours of meditation, or the devotional aspects – and may step back for a while.

What you believe and live by, judges you. The heroic style of the age is blackwashing, not whitewashing. One symptom is Christopher Hitchens's *The Missionary Position*, his demythologising of Mother Teresa's life-work – jacket-puffed as "hilariously mean". Hitchens's friend Martin Amis has written that Indian mysticism means the ability not to see Indian poverty. Our taste for bad news is inexhaustible, our best books – Lorna Sage's wonderful *Bad Blood*, Sebald's magnificent *Rings of Saturn* – always gloomy. As with Dostoevsky's *Underground Man*, nothing is so quick at awakening our disgust and active spite as any hint of idealism or transcendance.

The meditator can split into two contradictory people. One, an ordinary unregenerate impatient jaded materialist, sees humankind as a fortuitous and point-less blend of minerals and star-gases in a dead universe, and life as self-interested, without meaning. He is a cynic, which is to say a disappointed romantic. For him the spiritual path is pretentious, a kind of vanity. His favourite opening line is Beckett's *Murphy*: "The sun shone, having no alternative, on the nothing new" with its echo of *Ecclesiastes* ("Nothing new under the sun"); though he scorns all that is lyrical or elegiac.

His favourite adverb is Martin Amis's "unsur-prisingly". He fears his own disappearance, both in death, and in meditation. He resembles the hero in Sartre's novel *Nausea*, for whom the world exists in superabundant threat to his own sense of being. This stubborn hero is all too familiar, to the point sometimes of seeming almost to be part of me.

Yet this is not the whole story. An alternative persona has a child's capacity to lose itself in a condition of extreme wakefulness, attentive to what it sees or hears or does, "engrossed in a world of play". The perceptual

164

field expands and shows a new world: the mystic finds the meaning of life within love. There is no final victor in the war between these two embattled personae, and meditation is one site where they repeatedly encounter one another.

After extended meditation the joyous mystic is ascendant; in periods of idleness the depressed, anxious, cynic wins. They speak different tongues. The world appears very differently to each, with its own internally coherent logic. They seem zoologically distinct species, each addicted to his own cherished truths.

The mystic, however, does not see *more* than the cynic: he sees less. What is subtracted is what is self-involved. With that crucial subtraction, the world and all that it contains becomes vivid and marvellous and moving. The cynic suffers less impersonally. He is anxious, and depressive. It is remarked of some who are dying that they record their wonderment at never before having felt so intensely alive. The meditator would like to feel aliveness without being obliged to wait for this final moment. The terror of a world without sacredness is the greatest terror. The meditator remembers that life itself is sacred; the cynic forgets this.

***

Why do many persist with meditation, given the many pitfalls? Perhaps they become less anxious, or develop a more spacious quietness, energy and contentment, or a better heart, and feel that such qualities answer a private yearning: a simple, romantic belief – in the best sense – that developing compassion matters. Buddhism emphasises the essential workability of all situations, and that for the meditator obstacles might turn into challenges. Seeing fellow-practitioners discover resourcefulness is inspiring.

Retreat-practice is one place where such processes seem for a while accelerated and visible, and most Buddhist paths involve some form of retreat, solitary, or communal, or some alternation of both.

En route to my first month-long group retreat in August 1985, I reflected that I had hated public school: why did I put myself through replications of its conformism and absence of privacy, such as once spending a year working on a kibbutz, and now a long communal retreat?

Month-long group retreat is described, perhaps optimistically, as the "best present you can give yourself". It resembles being invited outside your life to understand the principles that secretly govern it.

Friends who have recovered from a stroke recount how "cobbled-together" their sense of self can suddenly come to seem. We are not what or who we think we are: we think ourselves into being. Nor is our world quite as solid as it sometimes looks, or rather, as we try to make it. The mind tries to solidify and freeze experience, to turn what is intrinsically fluid into a fixed story.

Month-long group retreat is sometimes also described as coming home to complete simplicity; a healing surrender to the contingency of things. (There are said to be three Buddhist lies, the first of which is "I enjoyed every minute of my month-long group retreat". The second is "I'm not jealous – despite the fact that my partner has gone off for the night"; the third, "The talk will begin promptly at eight o'clock".)

This first month-long group retreat happened near Drogheda in a red-brick ex-orphanage whose nineteenth-century Church-of-Ireland nurses had bullied and patronised Catholic single mothers. A mean-spirited depressing list of house-rules from around 1890 hung on one wall. Although most who meditated there loved the house and were heart-broken when it had later to be sold, I felt unhappiness enduring like wet-rot: it was always damp. It rained each and every day. Most slept in dorms.

I slept in a tiny tent with a bottle of illicit hooch for a night-cap and emerged, umbrella-forwards, when the bell sounded at 6.30 a.m. into a Somme of mud each morning.

There were days indoors when everyone seemed to be wading, metaphorically speaking, through deepest mud, too, and the going was hard. Close by on the same estate a twelfth-century tower survived from a ruined castle, at the ricketty top of which the demanding so-called "preliminary" practices happened. These start with 108,000 full prostrations, a surrender that can make you physically fit but also make you encounter your emotional volatility (the number 108 has special significance to Tibetan Buddhists).

Poisonous yellow ragwort beset the common approach-path, the water-supply was so limited that both baths and the flushing of the lavatories were rationed, and quarrelling farmers abounded. I was unsurprised that the place later turned into a themed hotel for Gothic Horror weekends. A gentle landscape undulated towards the ancient iron-age burial site of New Grange.

In nearby Drogheda Cathedral the withered black hand of the Blessed Oliver Plunkett, martyr of sacred memory, sat mesmerisingly in its glass case, a relic to be worshipped. We were twenty miles from the border, and the Troubles too. We joked that suspicious locals might say of us, "Who knows whether them feckers is *Catholic* Boodists or *Protestant* Boodists?" (I overheard one visitor whisper to her friend, "They don't *dress* like Noodists" and be answered, "Not *Noodists* eejit: *Boodists*.")

Our house-rules had their own rigours, which included a ban on alcohol, drugs, musical instruments and non-Buddhist books. There was often a rule of silence, so you adopted mime except when doing kitchen-work, where not speaking might cause dangers, and even there speaking was "functional" – "Pass the salt"– no chatter. We meditated for an hour before breakfast, then three hours before lunch, did house-chores followed by a free hour, then three hours "sitting" before dinner, and an hour or two afterwards. There was one wholly uninterrupted three-hour meditation session, unannounced, at the end of the month, a "tradition" that has since languished. The previous year the retreat leader, from Germany, clearly kept people meditating too late. From an empty shrine room, he eventually tracked down the practitioners sensibly, mutinously quaffing pub Guinness miles away. We were luckier in 1985: the going was easier.

Meals were eaten in silence, in the style of Zen monks, using a demanding ritual called *oryoki* that was, in prospect, terrifying. It was said that Trungpa Rinpoché observed his early students sitting well in meditation and then raiding the ice-box to eat like lower beings. He introduced *oryoki* as a bridge between meditation and "real life". This precise eating practice requires a choreography to develop mindfulness and awareness.

You are served, seated uncomfortably cross-legged only on your flat under-cushion, in quadrants, and the opening and closing of the lacquered set of nesting bowls with their blue ritual cloths have an exact decorum to each single movement, as has the manner in which it is served (with generosity) and, in principle, eaten (with elegance, without greed). Nothing is wasted.

The opening chants are so long that the food is invariably luke-warm by the time you get to eat it. You use chop-sticks. Chants aside, meals are entirely silent, and communication on being served is by *mudras* (hand-gestures) betokening "Only a small quantity" or "Enough" of each of three dishes. Then you clean your own set with hot water and drink the slops. After a week, fear went and was replaced by delight in high comedy. Each individual revealed himself nakedly in how he related to food: greedily, nonchalantly, or in ignorance.

It was soon hard to stop laughing. Watching 30 adults from half a dozen countries earnestly meditate seemed a good joke. Laughter came, too, from listening to good but solemn talks on "Obstacles to meditation and their Antidotes" (laziness, wildness &tc), "The Nine points of resting the Mind" and "The six marks of a Dharmic person" (cutting down too many activities, passionlessness: there was plenty of passion on the retreat, but clinging to passion is not enjoined). Laughter came from the realisation that nobody truly hides except from himself; it came unbidden at many points in the day, and irritated some German friends, though others minded *foux rires* less. Some wept in letting go of a life-time's tension instead, seeming to express the grief of beings everywhere.

But the effect was the same, a kind of letting go into the discipline of the day, and of moving through a pain barrier like Alice disappearing through the looking-glass.

On the far side of "pain" was a new world full of unexpected space and detail. You entered it by discovering that what you had feared as pain was not pain at all, or rather, was purely impersonal, a characteristic of how things always were, but which you had fortified and defended yourself against noticing. There was less need to insert a sense of self into the pain as a signature. "It suffers," rather than "I suffer," the Buddha said. Life was slowed down, and the volume turned up.

The journey between these two was marked by claustrophobia, by bodily aches and pains, by witnessing the compulsive and stale nature of much fantasy, where nothing fresh could happen. The tension of silence gradually changed into relaxation and relief. Here was a a precious commodity, lost and rediscovered.

You arrive with the speed of the ordinary world, so collisions occur, from which something is learnt. The ordinary judging/censorious mind holds the world at bay; the acceptant/relaxed mind welcomes the world as it is; and it is easier to ask changes of one's world if one is willing firstly to see it as it is. Willing it to differ changes nothing. One older woman arrived whose naked aggression pained many. It was revelatory to find the courage to confront her – after 9.30 at night, when ordinary speech was sometimes permitted – and then to learn to like her, too. Normally it is not always clear what emotion belongs to whom, and it is possible to feel somebody else's shame as if their frailty were yours.

Some sorting out seemed to have happened. Yet there were communal moods, too, both of elation and sorrow.

Benedick in *Much Ado about Nothing*, seeing his own flightiness, announces: "Man is a giddy thing; and that is my conclusion." The mind is giddier even than one suspected. You fall in love at sunrise, dislike the same person at lunch, feel indifferent at tea, and are in love again by dinner. You watch the tendency of mind to make "a mile out of an inch". It makes an Iris novel look understated. Since one is hollow, some humbleness follows. Here were new incentives to think about "emptiness".

I had no idea that a day had so much time packed into it. On a ten-day retreat soon after I was astonished to witness a drying-up cloth fall in slow motion. Doubtless it had always fallen at the same speed. My mind had slowed down to meet it.

Extended meditation discloses an experience of profound aloneness, and yet, in the middle of an intensely solitary and silent journey, a strong sense of community and genuine intimacy develop, and the birth of some compassion. Patience is said to be the key to all: the hardest of virtues especially to one ordinarily styled to win the competition for most impatient person in the room or on the planet. Patience is based (we are told) on physical relaxation. Not that it reveals a new world, but rather that it reveals the old world anew, so one sees what one's busy-ness earlier concealed. When Iris enquired about it later, I said, "You fall in love with everyone, even with those you hate" – a state of unrequited yet un-hungry love – and she laughed, then said, "So you sat on the ground? That's good."

Sometimes friends ask, "Is Buddhism escapist?" The Buddhist might answer that there are aspects of our existence worth escaping, in the sense of losing, or going beyond: neurotic misery; the uncomfortable egoistic anxiety delineated by the First Noble Truth which often drives us and at the same time keeps us asleep; those mental habits that freeze experience and lead us into error, hatred and greed, and which, writ large, threaten warfare and global ecological disaster.

"But isn't meditation life-denying, in the sense of joyless?" the questioner persists. If there were no happiness, no one would continue. "I am not afraid of such pleasures," the Buddha said. It seems, on the contrary, life-affirming, disclosing "our most intimate and secret life, its freedom, its abundant creativity, and its joy". On the contrary, it is our secular culture that, because it is death-denying, is by the same token life-denying and joyless. Fear of dying, and indeed of living, turn out to be closer than one had thought. Since then I've attended seven more such month-long retreats, and led a number myself.

***

After the Ecstasy, the Laundry is the title of one book about the difficulty of stabilising and inhabiting meditation experiences, which come and go and, for us, the unenlightened, are no more permanent than life-experiences generally. Temporary experiences met with during meditation (in Tibetan they are recognised as so commonplace as to merit a name: *nyams*) are to be worked with and let go, so that one does not get attached even to the happiest of them. Tibetans employ words designed specifically to dispel attachment to elated states, which presumably differ from the bliss of enlightenment itself. Possibly elation abstracts you from the present moment, while bliss locates you firmly within it. All the great Buddhist teachers are notably happy: presumably true of great Moslem, Jewish and Christian teachers too. It does sometimes seem that happy states linger longer when you are willing to relinquish them, and Suzuki Roshi writes more of enlightened "moments" than of enlightened beings, and suggests that even one's enlightened moments or glimpses should be let go of and treated as no big deal. States of elation, non-thought and clarity are properly regarded as temporary experiences if not distractions, because Westerners (especially) become fascinated by them, and then by their inevitable loss. They can none the less be memorable.

One recent November Jim and I were invited to Bhutan, the last Tibetan Buddhist kingdom on earth. Normally you pay a large sum to go trekking; we were fortunately guests and so exempt from daily charge. The small jet flies in between two Himalayan peaks at an exciting angle of 45 degrees on to its unnervingly short landing-strip. Driving is disconcerting: monsoon landslides can block the roads, and elsewhere and without warning, the highway abruptly stops, washed away down the valley towards India. The Bhutanese, by royal edict, wear quaint but workaday folk-costume. They are taught in English, which many speak, after a rough fashion, thanks to the diligence of a Canadian Jesuit who converted nobody, but is much remembered and much loved, and who set up the Bhutanese school-system.

Erect phalluses – fertility-symbols – are painted on the outside walls of many farmhouses, together with four animal symbols: tiger, snow-lion, the mythical garuda and dragon. Trungpa Rinpoché glossed these in his writings as the dignities or colours of enlightened mind, explicating their secret meaning poetically as representing different, and successively deeper, manifestations of egolessness. It was remarkable to see these potent symbols in their own Himalayan habitat.

Remarkable, too, to meet Nyoshul Rinpoché, a great once-mendicant lama since deceased, who interrupted a many-hours-long group practice with his monks and also his dogs sitting side-by-side on brocaded cushions to offer us an interview we had not dreamt of soliciting. He asked us what questions we had for him, and when we were awkwardly silent, appeared to roll his eyes up and back into their sockets, so that only the whites showed, and unnervingly addressed with great accuracy what was in our hearts and undisclosed. We held few surprises for him.

We drove to the monastery of Ganté and negotiated use of a simple retreat cabin at 11,000 feet overlooking mountains vigorously fluttering everywhere with prayer-flags where we cooked disgusting wood-smoke-ridden, vegetarian, campfire meals, took water from a spring we shared with yaks, had mild altitude sickness – headaches, difficulties sleeping from breathlessness – and meditated for some days.

Ganté monastery way below resembled a small gold-roofed Tibetan palace; one of its compounds contained monks in three-year retreat. Golden eagle soared overhead. Garrulous parties of chough, one kind red-beaked, the other orange, flew playfully in and out of the eaves of the cabin, chattering noisily – an indescribable shooting arrow-like sound, sometimes recalling a choir manically plucking at the treble notes of broken pianos.

Black-necked cranes sailed slowly over from Lhasa. There are just 5,000 of these left, and each has a seven-foot wingspan, and spends the winter exclusively in Ladakh, and in this one valley in Bhutan, where their annual landing on strange stilted legs provokes a festival with lamas dancing. The cranes are creatures of good omen. They pass overhead with a haunting, melancholy, falling, three-note cry, as if attuned to grief.

Our nights were cheered by the excellent whisky the gentle Bhutanese distil. Himalayan night-skies are dazzling, for there is no light-pollution anywhere, and we were high. Vast, immensely brilliant star-populations turn slowly above. They induce awe, stop the mind, and open the heart.

One such night I pondered the old needling questions that can rightly elicit only what George Meredith called "a dusty answer": "How is there a world, something rather than nothing?... What *sense* is to be found?"

A story I had heard when living in Poland for two years, a story touching some deep nerves, came back unbidden. When asked "Who are you?", a Warsaw friend's house-keeper replied that she did not know. She knew only that her mother was rounded up for deportation in Warsaw's *Umschlagplatz* around 1943.

By this stage in the war it was understood that this meant a cattle-truck to the gas-chambers of Treblinka, and most knew how soon and in what manner that journey would end. In the square the terrified, ill-nourished women from the ghetto passed their babies over their heads from one to another set of upraised hands – as I saw it in my mind's eye, with care, though presumably also with haste – towards a high wall enclosing them. They were thrown over to the far side, where pious Catholic Polish women waited and caught, collected and brought them up as gentiles.

This tale haunted me, as if it contained the key to understanding something else. This woman did not know who she was. She knew only that she was the child of two kinds of courage: that of a forever nameless mother who had let her go, and that of a foster-mother, who held and cherished her.

Her story was scarcely universal. Yet it seemed to shed its own strange light. There might never be final answers to the old questions. But meanwhile the qualities both mother and foster-mother alike showed on that singular day were as palpable as life itself: both had lived in the challenge and intensity of the moment, rather than among imponderables. There are sources of terror, but courage, generosity and compassion are real too.

Like the Himalayan night-sky, the story stops my mind.

***

I remember a different night on a month-long retreat. Meditation can (but need not) unlock joyous states, better even than the joy of sex with someone you deeply love. Because one is, albeit momentarily, in the truth, a state of compassion so hair-triggered that you can watch one grown man shed tears on one side of the meditation room, while a second, witnessing him from the other side of the room, visibly feels for the first... Yet you are absolutely your own person, and like yourself and you have the power to bless and to be blessed. Self-consciousness and embarrassment go; a grace of certainty replaces them. How can that be? You belong to yourself, as if for the first time, and then notice how naturally that self feels for others. Everyone, it seems clear, carries her or his own wisdom, though they have not yet always understood this...

You are in love and broken-hearted, but without any drunken or blind need, the exact opposite of depressed. If you are drunk at all it is on looking at others and their beauty. Those who have meditated for a month look beautiful, ten years younger, newly-fledged. You can recognise them in a meditation centre. It is said that they appear processed by discipline, both mindful and aware... You need nothing and nobody and have discovered (for a spell) how to be quiet and still and that much speech is superfluous, un-mindful, and you are in love with the world and all that it contains, and see how valuable, fragile and painfully moving that world is, like a cosmonaut witnessing for the first time the little globe journeying nakedly, vulnerably, bravely through open space, with its infinitely precious serendipitous cargo.

You are quietly and as if as never before certain of your own mortality, and that of others, not resenting "the contract" under the terms of which all humans suffer and labour. There is gratitude instead, and a sense of power. For example, the power to glimpse Yeats's understanding that the soul is "self-delighting/ self-appeasing, self-affrighting" and then the power physically to touch – to those brought up in stuffy English boarding-schools, a real discovery

At a last-night bonfire-party on that first month-long group retreat an Irish friend recited Prospero from memory and was asked to repeat and repeat the whole speech by the others, most of whose first language was not English (Dutch, German, French), listening spellbound, as the sparks flew upward into the night-sky:

> Our revels now are ended. These our actors,
> As I foretold you, were all spirits and
> Are melted into air, into thin air:
> And, like the baseless fabric of this vision,
> The cloud-topped towers, the gorgeous palaces,
> The solemn temples, the great globe itself,
> Yea, all which it inherit, shall dissolve
> And, like this insubstantial pageant faded,
> Leave not a rack behind. We are such stuff

As dreams are made on, and our little life
Is rounded with a sleep...

A friend, a tough-looking postman, observed humorously of his fellow-meditators, "I don't know why I'm crying; *I've hated them all for the whole month.*"

I imagine the scorn of a cynical friend and want to say to him that this joy is not stupid or soft but tough and intelligent even if short-lived. It fades and the beginner wants it back. If there is intelligence within cynicism (and there is), there is also soured romanticism. The cynic's secret hope is that his is not the whole story; his secret fear that it is. His is *not* the whole story, though giving up cynicism is frightening: it protects from feeling.

I tried to explain all this later to Iris, repeating, "You fall in love with everyone, even with the people that you hate," and she laughed, and then thought carefully in her customary way, and watched as a dog watches, and replied gently and firmly: "That's good."

BRIEF BIBLIOGRAPHY

This study is greatly indebted to the work and thoughts of others. Among them:

S.Z. Suzuki, *Zen Mind, Beginner's Mind* (1970)

Chögyam Trungpa, *Cutting Through Spiritual Materialism* (1973)

Shambhala, Sacred Path of the Warrior (1984)

Willard Johnson, *Riding the Ox Home* (1982)

Edward Conze, *A Short History of Buddhism* (1980)

Andrew Harvey, *A Journey in Ladakh* (1983)

Paul Williams, *Mahayana Buddhism* (1989)

Peter Harvey, *An Introduction to Buddhism* (1990)

Rick Fields, *How the Swans Came to the Lake: A Narrative History of Buddhism in America* (1992)

Geoffrey Samuel, *Civilised Shamans* (1993)

Stephen Batchelor, *The Awakening of the West: the encounter of Buddhism and Western Culture* (1994)

Mark Epstein, *Thoughts without a Thinker* (1997), *Going on Being* (2001)

Donald Lopez, *Prisoners of Shangri-La: Tibetan Buddhism and the West* (1998)

Reginald Ray, *Indestructible Truth: The Living*

Spirituality of Tibetan Buddhism (2000)

Michael Downing, *Shoes outside the Door* (2001)

Sakyong Mipham, *Turning the Mind into an Ally* (2002)

Patrick French, *Tibet, Tibet* (2003)

I also benefited much from the comments of Paul Binding, Bill Hamilton, Tony Garrett, Jane Jantet, Mary Midgley, Jim O'Neill, Adam Phillips, Rob Puts, Anne Roberts, David Schneider, Daphne Turner, and Han de Wit.